BOMBER COUNTY

A HISTORY OF THE ROYAL AIR FORCE IN LINCOLNSHIRE

LINCOLNSHIRE HISTORY SERIES

1 ENGLISH J S   '. . . AND ALL WAS LIGHT'
                    Isaac Newton — 1977

2 HANCOCK T N   'BOMBER COUNTY'
                    A History of the Royal Air Force in
                    Lincolnshire — 1978

Front cover

The two aircraft types most associated with Lincolnshire. The RAFs last flying Avro Lancaster, PA 474, of the Battle of Britain Memorial Flight, Coningsby, and Avro Vulcan B2, XL 317 of 617 (The Dambusters) Sdn, Scampton, formate over Lincoln Cathedral, a welcome landmark to thousands of RAF aircrew.

Cover by Carter Daffern Design.

BOMBER COUNTY

A HISTORY OF
THE ROYAL AIR FORCE
IN
LINCOLNSHIRE

by

T N HANCOCK

Lincolnshire
Library Service

Lincolnshire History Series No 2

Lincolnshire Library Service,
Brayford House, Lucy Tower Street,
Lincoln.

First published 1978
2nd impression 1978
3rd impression 1980
Reprinted with minor revision 1982
4th impression 1984
5th impression 1989
Reprinted with minor revisions

ISBN 0 86111 100 1

Printed and bound by G. W. Belton Ltd., Gainsborough.

Contents

Illustrations

Foreword

Introduction

Part one
World War I   1
    Royal Naval Air Service   1
    Royal Flying Corps — Home defence   8
    Royal Flying Corps — Training   11
    Royal Air Force — Anti-submarine patrols   16

Part two
Between the Wars   17
    The RAF College   17
    The Flying Training Schools   23
    Operational Flying   29

Part three
World War II — The early years 1939-1942   35
    Fighter operations   36
    Bomber operations   45
    Coastal Command   50
    Training   52

Part four
World War II — the later years 1943-1945   57
    Bomber operations   57
    Bomber support   74
    Bomber training   75
    Fighter operations   76
    Coastal Command   78
    Flying training   80
    Non-flying units   82
    The Americans   84
    The reckoning   87

Part five
The post war years 1945-1978   89
    The run down   89
    The first jets 1951-1955   90
    Training 1945-1955   92
    The nuclear deterrent   95
    Air defence 1955-1978   100
    Training 1955-1978   104

Part six
Where were they?   112

Bibliography..   134

Index   138

Illustrations

Page

1 A DFW biplane near Grimsby 3
2 Avro 504A of HMS Daedalus 6
3 The airship station at Cranwell c1917 7
4 Personnel of A Flight, 33 Sdn, at Kirton-in-Lindsey, 1918 10
5 RE7 at Harlaxton, 1917 13
6 South Carlton airfield, 1918 14
7 The Motor Transport section at Cranwell in 1919 18
8 De Havilland DH9A two seat trainer 20
9 Armstrong-Whitworth Siskins at Cranwell 21
10 The first six pilots of the Royal Indian Air Force training at Cranwell 22
11 Hawker Hart Trainers at Digby 24
12 Training aircraft at Waltham, Grimsby 25
13 A Fairey Gordon over Donna Nook range 27
14 Westland Wallaces over the Lincolnshire coast 27
15 A Fairey Fawn light bomber of 503 Sdn 28
16 A Handley-Page Hinaidi of 503 Sdn 29
17 Fatal crash at Waddington, February 1937 30
18 Handley-Page Heyford force landed at Donna Nook 32
19 Gloster Gladiators at Digby, 1938 33
20 Handley-Page Hampdens over Lincoln Cathedral 34
21 Gravestone of P/O John Gillespie Magee 40
22 A Hampden of 50 Sdn at Swinderby 47
23 50 Sdn Avro Manchester, 1942 49
24 'St Vincents' Grantham, 5 Group HQ 59
25 World War II Lancaster crew, 617 Sdn 63
26 A Lancaster of 101 Sdn showing ABC aerials 64
27 The mighty Lancaster. G-George, veteran of 126 ops 67
28 Coleby Grange control tower 77
29 Summer 1944 — at Goxhill 84
30 USAAF C47 Dakotas 86
31 Lively Lincoln! . . . airborne from Binbrook 88
32 101 Sdn Lincoln over Cleethorpes 88
33 The first Canberra at Binbrook, 1951 91
34 Tiger Moths at Kirton-in-Lindsey 94
35 Record breaking Vulcan, XA897, at Khormaksar 96
36 Vulcan B2 in low level camouflage 98
37 Hastings T5, TG517, of '1066 Sdn' 230 OCU 100
38 Canberra WD 948 in a new role 101
39 BAC Lightning F6 in original natural finish 102
40 29 Sdn Phantom crew 103
41 The current Lincolnshire aerobatic team 'The Poachers' 105
42 'City of Lincoln' Lancaster PA 474 109
43 BAC Lightning F6 in camouflage 110
44 World War I hangars at Bracebridge Heath 113
45 Aircraft of 3 FTS at Grantham in 1934 118
46 'Mudford Magna' during the winter 122

47 Hunting Jet Provost T4s of the 'Macaws' 122
48 North Coates airfield, 1937 124
49 27 Sdn Vulcan, Scampton 126
50 A Westland Wallace of 503 Sdn 128
      Plans Lincolnshire RAF Stations World War I 132
             Lincolnshire RAF Stations World War II 133
             Fiskerton airfield key and fold-out map 142

FOREWORD

by

AIR VICE-MARSHAL D HARCOURT-SMITH DFC RAF

AIR OFFICER COMMANDING AND COMMANDANT

ROYAL AIR FORCE COLLEGE CRANWELL

The concept of a modern air force such as the Royal Air Force having roots might be considered to be an incongruity; nevertheless, if the Royal Air Force has roots anywhere it has them in Lincolnshire.

In this book the author recounts with clarity, humour and compassion the story of the men and women of the Royal Air Force, who for a time made Lincolnshire their home and took to their hearts its people. Although the story covers in great detail the formations and aircraft of the Royal Air Force which have been located in Lincolnshire, the book is essentially about people, the predecessors of the men and women of today's Royal Air Force who proudly nurture its roots long established in the friendly soil of this county.

Introduction

It's simple for a visitor to Lincoln to identify a native of the City — he or she doesn't look up when a Waddington Vulcan turns noisily in the circuit 2,000 feet overhead! An apocryphal story perhaps, but Lincolnshire folk have been used to flying machines since 1914, when they were a rarity in most other parts of Britain. Since that date, there have always been RAF stations in Lincolnshire and the Service has played a large part in the recent history of the county especially during World War II, when it was indeed a 'bomber county'. In this book I have tried to capture the flavour of the different periods by including excerpts from books written by airmen serving in the county which, incidentally, I have taken as the pre-1974 area. The major part of the book is in narrative form, and this is followed by an alphabetical list of Lincolnshire RAF Stations with brief details of units based at them. In such a brief history it is only possible to record salient details, but any reader who can fill gaps, correct any information, or provide photographs for copying, is asked to contact the author direct at Lincolnshire Library Service HQ.

Acknowledgements

While writing this book I have been overwhelmed by the generous help given by many people; in particular I would like to thank — Group Captain Dowling and Flt Lt Brian Ferrill, RAF Swinderby; Sdn Ldr Tait, Flt Lt Ken Edmunds (11 Sdn) and F/O Peter Stone (5 Sdn), RAF Binbrook; Flt Lt John Rees and Flt Lt Wade (50 Sdn), Flt Lt Des Goff (101 Sdn), RAF Waddington; P/O Gillian Foy, RAF Nocton Hall; Flt Lt Gray, RAF Donna Nook; Flt Lt Sneller, RAF Holbeach; Flt Lt Curtis, RAF Wainfleet; Jean King, College Librarian, RAF Cranwell; CRO, RAF Scampton; Flt Lt Weaver, RAF Coningsby; Trevor Muhl (ex 207 and 617 Sdns); Vicki Muhl (ex WAAF); Harold Willars (ex 503 Sdn); Perry Sparkes (ex 33 Sdn); Public Records Office, Kew; Air Historical Branch, Ministry of Defence; Fleet Air Arm Museum; RAF Museum; Flight International; 1361st Audio Visual Sdn, USAF: RAF Inspectorate of Recruiting Photographic Library; John Walls; Peter Green; Dave Langlands; those publishers who have allowed me to quote from various books; Fran Cooper for typing; Owen Northwood for editing and lastly AV-M David Harcourt-Smith for writing a foreword.

T N Hancock
Lincoln.
June 1978.

Part One

World War One

The road signs which welcome travellers to Aldershot, Hampshire, name it the 'Home of the British Army', and certainly most people would connect Aldershot with the Army, as they would Catterick and Salisbury Plain. Similarly, mention of the Royal Navy conjures up Portsmouth and Plymouth to the Englishman; but what of the Royal Air Force whose history only goes back to early this century? Any list of counties thought of as connected with the RAF must include Lincolnshire, and its claim to be the 'Home of the RAF' has increased steadily over the years until it cannot, in 1978, be disputed. The county based squadrons, seven Vulcan, two Lightning and one Phantom, total over 25% of the RAFs combat squadrons; all airmen recruits to the Service pass through Swinderby; and all career officers pass through Cranwell. Historically, Lincolnshire had more airfields (45) during World War II than any other county, Yorkshire and Norfolk being second and third in the league. Perhaps it is time our county road signs proclaimed 'Lincolnshire — home of the Royal Air Force'.

Royal Naval Air Service

However, the county cannot claim to be the birthplace of the RAF as the first airfields of its antecedents, the Royal Flying Corps and Royal Naval Air Service, were established around military training areas at Netheravon, Upavon and Farnborough for example, or near naval ports, as were Eastchurch and Gosport. In August 1913 the Admiralty issued orders promulgating several coastal air stations of which Newcastle was the principal, with Cleethorpes and Great Yarmouth as subcommands; in fact, neither Newcastle nor Cleethorpes air stations materialized and, at the outbreak of war in August 1914, the RN had organised a system of aerial patrols around the coast based on eight seaplane stations — Calshot, Dundee, Eastchurch, Felixstowe, Fort Grange (Portsmouth), Isle of Grain, Killingholme and Great Yarmouth.

1

On 10 August 1914, Wing Commander Samson, a famous pioneer airman of the RNAS, was ordered to establish a base at Skegness and take charge of air patrols from the Humber to Cromer, including the defence of the Admiralty fuel tanks at Immingham. Three patrols were flown daily from Skegness during its brief existence. Patrol A was Skegness — Cleethorpes — Mablethorpe — Skegness; Patrol B Skegness — Cromer — Skegness; and Patrol C Skegness — six miles north of Mablethorpe — Skegness — the Wash — Skegness.

Killingholme soon replaced Skegness, flying its first patrol on 21 August, the camp itself being a very makeshift affair. It was December before hutted accommodation was provided and the road to the station metalled. A typical patrol flown in the early war years from Killingholme was that of Flt Sub-Lt Adams, on 18 November 1914. (The aircraft type is given as a DFW, a German biplane purchased by the Admiralty pre-war). He

' . . . left Killingholme at 0730, turned at Donna Nook 0810, landed Killingholme 0845. Altitude 2,000 ft, vis 10 m, weather good, conditions some showers. Wind 10 mph. Area clear'.

Bad weather, of course, stopped flying. Various aircraft were flown in these early days, some with strange names including Sopwith Spinning Jennies, Schneiders and Babies, Short 827s and White & Thompson Bognor Bloaters.

Cdr A H Longmore took over command in 1916.

'On June 15th 1916 I took over command of Killingholme, where some recently built sheds were waiting to house the new large American flying boats which had not yet been delivered. Short float seaplanes with single 225 h.p. Sunbeam engines and a few Sopwith Scout seaplanes were in use, the former for patrols and the latter for interception of Zeppelins. Up to date they had not been very successful, and it was not a very well placed station for operating seaplanes on account of the strong tide in the estuary and the large rise and fall which made slipway work difficult. . . .

1   *A DFW biplane of the RNAS in a Grimsby field while on its way to Killing-*
holme in 1914. This German type was withdrawn from service soon after the
start of WWI, because of identification problems. (Humberside Libraries).

Zeppelins were very active over the North Sea of England about this time. In
August there was a report that ten of them were out, evidently scouting for
some enterprise by the German High Sea Fleet. Flt Lt Fox managed to reach
one in his Sopwith Scout off Spurn Head and damaged it. There were night
raids on Hull and Grimsby; the technique of bringing them down at night had
not yet developed and none of our machines were fitted for night flying.

Two paddle-wheel minesweepers were fitted to carry two Sopwith Scout
seaplanes each. The idea was that the craft would be out at the entrance to the
Humber at their usual work of sweeping for mines but in the evening would
hoist out the seaplanes. These would take off and patrol for Zeppelins which
were, rather blatantly, making a landfall before dark to locate their position
for subsequent night operation. The Sopwith Scouts did not come into action
whilst I was there, but the idea was quite good'.

(Longmore A *From Sea to Sky* Bles 1946)

Actually, one converted paddle steamer, HMS Killingholme, carrying
two Sopwith Schneider seaplanes, was based at Killingholme. The large
American flying boats mentioned by Cdr Longmore were possibly the
Curtis-Wanamaker Triplane, which in fact never arrived at Killingholme. American flying boats did arrive however, in 1917 in the shape

3

of the Curtis H4 Small America, which saw service at most RNAS stations. By this time Killingholme had become one of the leading seaplane stations, though landplanes were also based there. Its complement was 900 sailors and it was used for training seaplane pilots as well as its operational duties. At times there were as many as 100 machines there. September 1916 saw several Zeppelin raids on Lincolnshire — L22 crossed the coast at Skegness and bombed Humberston, L13 came in over Spurn Head and dropped bombs at Owmby and Gainsborough, then caused serious damage at East Retford, while L23 bombed Boston. This was the biggest Zeppelin raid of the war and Killingholme aircraft were airborne trying to intercept, as they were for many other raids in 1916. Later the Small America was joined by the H12 Large America and these boats performed both anti-sub and anti-Zeppelin patrols far out over the North Sea to the Danish coast. Both the US boats suffered from poor seaworthiness and an RN Officer, John Porte, redesigned the hull of the H4, thus giving rise to the excellent Felixstowe F2 which performed sterling work for the rest of the war. Short 184s and 320s also served at the station.

From March 1918 US Navy airmen began to appear and the last British CO was W/C F Bowhill (later AM Sir Fredk Bowhill); 20 July 1918 saw the station transferred to the United States Navy. Operations flown by the Americans were convoy escort, submarine search, long distance reconnaissance and special patrols in response to warnings of approaching enemy air or sea craft. In the period from their takeover to the Armistice 233 flights were undertaken, these averaging 4 hours 10 minutes each. (From February-July 1918 the RNAS had flown 1,095 hours in 301 flights). The USN handed Killingholme back to the British in January 1919, when the Large Americas of 228 Sdn RAF arrived from Yarmouth. This squadron disbanded in June 1919 and 249 Sdn with Short 184 seaplanes disbanded in October, after which Killingholme closed down.

Just down the coast at Immingham the RNAS had established 8 Kite Balloon Section. Kite balloons were similar to the RFCs observation balloons, having a wicker basket slung beneath for the crew; when trailed from convoy escorts at 3,000 ft, the horizon visible was 63 miles in clear weather and the observer watched for mines, torpedo tracks, submarines and, if necessary, spotted for gunners. Balloons from 8 KBS equipped the Humber based escorts and one of its balloon observers spotted a mine 10 ft below the surface in July 1918. Otherwise Immingham balloons had no great claim to fame, though kite balloons were responsible for the sinking of two U-boats during the war. From 1 April 1918 Immingham, like Killingholme, became part of the RAF and was known as 8 Balloon Station.

4

The RNAS had other 'stone frigates' in Lincolnshire. During 1915 Rear Admiral Vaughan-Lee put forward a plan to centralise RNAS training on seaplanes, balloons and airships. Cranwell was selected for three reasons — it had lots of room for expansion, newly qualified pilots could be posted easily to the RNAS east coast air stations and there were no outstanding natural features which would act as guides to enemy raiders. An advance party arrived on the 3,000 acre site in December 1915 and the RNAS Training Establishment, HMS Daedalus, opened on 1 April 1916, the first Commandant being Cdr Godfrey Paine RN. It was an enormous camp even by today's standards, with two airfields, one north of the camp and one south. On the northern edge of North Airfield was the airship station, the first shed for a kite balloon being completed in March 1916. In May the first free balloons arrived from Wormwood Scrubs, one SS (Sea Scout) Airship crashing near Sleaford during the move. The large rigid-airship shed came into use in June 1917 and eventually there were two large sheds and three small ones. The station in 1916 was still having many new buildings added and conditions were primitive. In Daedalus' magazine *Piloteer* it was suggested in 1917 that

'In view of the wholesale roadway and pathway improvements on the Station, a selected area of the true, original, MUD we have known and endured should be preserved and perpetuated in a framework of glass'.

So large was Cranwell that a single track railway was built from the main line at Sleaford — it was completed in 1917 and used by two locomotives, built by Manning and Wardle. The railway station is now the main guardroom, but the line was not finally removed until 1957, by which time a diesel locomotive was working it. Perhaps the railway helped to alleviate the problems of the sailor who wrote a lament sold on postcards at Cranwell in 1916, the first verse of which ran

"There's an isolated, desolated spot I'd like to mention,
Where all you hear is 'stand at ease', 'quick march', slope arms',
 'attention'.
It's miles away from anywhere, by jove it's a rum 'un,
A man lived there for 50 years and never saw a woman".

Be that as it may, King George V and Queen Mary visited the camp in July 1916. Apart from flying training there was also an Electrical and Wireless School, a Boys' Training Wing and a Physical Training School. The large influx of sailors had the expected effect on surrounding Lincolnshire and *Piloteer* recorded the first RNAS wedding at Sleaford when, on 16 June 1917, CPO 'Taff' Gibbons married an un-named bride at Quarrington Church and the happy couple were towed through the streets by a party of Petty Officers.

2 *Avro 504A, 2930, of HMS Daedalus, Cranwell, seen after a heavy landing c1917. Note the differing serial number on fin, indicating a previous accident.* (Capt D S Glover, via P H T Green).

Flt Sub-Lt Rochford describes the training he received at Cranwell.

'The day after my arrival I reported to Flt Lt A R Cox who was in charge of the Avro Flight on the North Aerodrome. Although I had already flown solo for nearly two hours on the Avros at Chingford, Cox took me up for a dual control flight to satisfy himself that I was competent. We landed after 25 minutes in the air and two days later I made three solo flights. After a further five flights, on one of which I made a spiral descent from 5,000 feet, I was transferred to the Curtiss Flight commanded by Flt Lt R B Munday on the South Aerodrome . . . . Towards the end of August, Munday took me up one evening for three short flights and on the third one we practised landing in a field adjoining the aerodrome. Two days later, following some further circuits and landings with Munday, I was allowed to fly the Curtiss solo for the first time'.

Rochford was then moved to the BE2c Flight and after familiarizing himself with the type —

'I flew my first cross-country, a compass and map reading course, Horncastle, Skegness and Freiston, landing at the aerodrome at Freiston, and later returning direct to Cranwell. The following day, in the morning, I made another cross-country flight to Bourne, Sutton Bridge, Boston and back to Cranwell'.

The last hurdle was training on the Bristol Scout, a fighter which had been replaced in France by more modern types, and then Rochford received his 'Wings'.

'From Cranwell I attended a short course at the bombing and gunnery school at Freiston where Flt Lt Morrison was the CO. This was a small RNAS Station under the control of Cranwell and was situated at the mouth of the Wash, the bombing being carried out in BE2c's on its large area of sandy beach. There were three stages in the bombing course: first, flying over the mirror; secondly, dropping dummy bombs; thirdly, dropping live bombs. The gunnery course was entirely on ground ranges'.

(Rochford E H *I chose the sky* Kimber 1977)

Despite Flt Sub-Lt Rochford's fairly accident free progress, learning to fly was still a dangerous business as the following record of fatal crashes at Cranwell shows from July 1917 to November 1918 — July, 3 killed in airship accident; August 2; October 1; December 2; January 2; February 1; March 4; April 2; May 3 (including 1 at Freiston); June 2; July 7 (including 2 USN); August 5; October 2; November 2. Not only were pilots at risk, as in June 1918 a mechanic was killed by a propellor.

3   The airship station at Cranwell, c1917. Note the enormous windbreak fences, the gas tanks, and the small airship over the large shed. (RAF Cranwell).

On 1 April 1918, the RNAS was merged with the RFC to form the RAF. This historic event seemed to pass the affected sailors and soldiers by;

'The first act of the great amalgamation has been witnessed, and, really, there was nothing fearfully exciting about it. On the first of April the Flagstaff flew a different pennon, but no mysterious and abrupt transition into khaki had occurred. We were all quite normal — members of the RAF in the habiliments (or togs) of the RNAS'.

Piloteer April 1918.

Different uniforms were present from November 1917 to April 1918, when a USN detachment was based at Cranwell.

Royal Flying Corps — Home Defence

The Zeppelin raids over Britain during 1915 caused much concern among the civilian population, and though by the end of 1916 the attacks by Zeppelins were rare, the Germans developed long range bomber aircraft — the Gothas, LVGs and Zeppelin-Stakens. However these bombers raided London and the South of England, and it was the Zeppelin airships which troubled the east coast. Slow, unwieldly and highly inflammable, the 'Zepps' nevertheless flew over England for as long as eight or nine hours, dropping bombs at random. As Lincolnshire, clearly defined by the Humber and the Wash, was a favourite entry point it received its share of raids, bombs falling at such diverse places as Humberston, East Halton, Alford, Anderby, Fiskerton, Uffington, Welbourn, Skellingthorpe and Metheringham. These caused little damage generally, but a lucky hit on an army billet at Cleethorpes on 1 April 1916 killed 31 soldiers of the Manchester Regiment. To counter these threats the War Office established a Home Defence network of aircraft, anti-aircraft guns and searchlights which took over air defence duties from RNAS stations like Killingholme. The Home Defence squadrons were initially equipped with aircraft which were obsolescent for service in France, mainly the ubiquitous BE2 and Avro 504, and covered the whole of the eastern side of Britain. Each squadron had an HQ and workshop which at first were in hired accommodation in a town, with three flights, one at each of three different airfields in the area around the HQ. Additionally landing grounds were dotted around the countryside, being usually a field with a shed for a couple of mechanics and a few flares which could be lit for emergency landings. This gives a clue to the problem, for the 'Zepps' came by night and so the HD squadrons also had to fly by night. It is difficult to imagine what courage must have been needed by these pilots, for there was no radio or radar and only very primitive flying instruments — but fly they did, and were so successful that the Zeppelins were withdrawn from raids on Britain, the last raid being on 5 August 1918.

Three Home Defence Squadrons had bases in Lincolnshire. 38 Sdn with FE2b's moved its HQ to Melton Mowbray, Leicestershire, in September 1916. Its three flights were stationed at Stamford (later called Wittering and thus in Northants), Buckminster, Leicestershire (though the airfield itself was in Lincolnshire), and Leadenham. The 'Fees' operated until May 1918 without once intercepting a Zeppelin. An interesting link with the county is that the CO in 1916/17 was Major Twistleton-Wykeham-Fiennes, a relation of the present Dean of Lincoln. 38 Sdn was replaced at Buckminster and Leadenham by 90 Sdn with Avro 504s and Dolphins; HQ was at Buckminster, A Flight at Leadenham and the unit disbanded in June 1919. The next link north in the HD chain was 33 Sdn which in December 1916 formed its HQ at Gainsborough where there was only a small landing ground, just across the Trent, into which squadron aircraft flew for major maintenance by the Squadron workshop. 33 Sdn FE2b's and d's were actually based at Brattleby, later to be called Scampton (A Flight), Kirton-in-Lindsey (B Flight) and Elsham (C Flight). Again it was their presence, rather than any action, which defeated the air raids although 33 was airborne, weather permitting, against every raid which took place against the Lincolnshire coast. In June 1918 the Squadron HQ moved to Kirton-in-Lindsey, and there it remained until disbanded in June 1919, having re-equipped with Bristol Fighters and Avro 504 night fighters.

Mr Perry Sparkes of Kempston, Bedfordshire, was the 33 Squadron armoury sergeant, also responsible for ground gunnery training. He recalls

'We were under canvas until Christmas Eve when we were stationed in a wing of Gainsborough workhouse, (very gruesome!). There was quite a lot of flying done at night but not many Zeppelin alerts. Each Flight was given a certain area to patrol in training. I do not remember any Zeppelins sighted in Lincoln. One night, with one of the very few alerts, an officer pilot with his gunner took an old FE2 up and crashed before leaving the landing ground; he, the pilot, was burnt to death and his gunner, a young 2nd Lt, sustained a broken collar bone but he followed the pilot to the grave next morning, the pilot being a Jew. We were very well treated by the Gainsborough people, so much so that quite a few of our chaps found wives in and around Gainsborough, myself included. My wife had two brothers, both chemists in the town, but she lived at Kirton, her father being a chemist, N Boon, a well known citizen of North Lincolnshire.

You query in your letter why was our HQ in Gainsborough and not at a flight station. The only reason I can account for this was it was much more comfortable and convenient than out on a flight station'.

Mr Sparkes was a founder member of 33 Sdn when it formed at Filton, Bristol, in January 1916, under Major Joubert, later ACM Sir Philip Joubert. Apart from its main Home Defence role 33 Sdn also trained pilots and observers in night flying, supplying large numbers of these to squadrons in France. US Army pilots were also trained for night flying, and C Flight co-operated with the artillery batteries at Spurn Head and Kilnsea. In the south of the county 51 Sdn, with HQ at Marham, Norfolk, had its most northerly Flight, B Flight, at Tydd St Mary where the aircraft were Avro 504 night fighters and later Camels. Again little action was recorded. Emergency landing grounds in the county used by the HD squadrons were at Anwick, Braceby, Bucknall, Cuxwold, Cockthorne, Gosberton, Grimsthorpe, Kelstern, Market Deeping, Moorby, New Holland, Swinstead and Winterton.

4   *Personnel of A Flight, 33 Sdn, at Scampton, March 1918. A large proportion are from the US Army Aviation Service — those wearing 'Mountie' style hats.* (Perry Sparkes).

Royal Flying Corps — Training

In early 1916 the RFC was greatly expanding — urgently required new squadrons were forming and pilots were needed for these. In addition the RFC was badly in need of replacement pilots as casualties began to mount on the Western Front largely due to the appearance of the Fokker Eindeckers, a monoplane fitted with a machine gun firing through the propellor, which could be aimed by line of flight. The RFC had no immediate answer to this, and the slow two-seater reconnaissance aircraft, mainly BE2c's, were easy prey for the Fokkers. The situation improved in the spring of 1916 when some RFC squadrons equipped with the Airco DH2 arrived in France, but in July the RFC was thrown into the Battle of the Somme and when this ended in November had lost nearly 700 pilots and observers. Training airfields and units were thus desperately needed and Lincolnshire's open countryside, sparse population and lack of industrial haze soon came to the notice of the airfield planners, as did the Lincoln escarpment — it is no accident that many of the World War I airfields were situated along the Cliff, where the prevailing south west wind gave added lift to aid take-off. Flying training had by this stage of the war progressed to a more formal programme compared with the early days. Trainee pilots were sent to Reserve Squadrons where they were required to fly a minimum number of fifteen hours solo, carry out some night flying and also receive instruction and practice in bombing, air fighting and formation flying.

In November 1916 five of these Reserve Squadrons moved into newly opened airfields in Lincolnshire; 37 Reserve Squadron at Scampton, 44 at Harlaxton, 45 at South Carlton, 47 at Waddington and 49 at Spitalgate. The aircraft were a mixture of Avro 504s, BE2s, Maurice Farmans, and Armstrong Whitworth FK3s. December saw a further increase in pilot qualifications when the minimum hours required to be flown solo were raised to 20 to 28 depending on the type of aircraft.

The Lincolnshire Reserve Squadrons came under the control of Northern Group Command at York and in May 1917 it was realized that the title Reserve Squadron was not entirely suitable, so they were renamed Training Squadrons. Some units were posted out and replaced by different Training Squadrons, but the training remained the same until the advent of the methods pioneered by Major Smith-Barry at the School of Special Flying, Gosport. These were the basis of the flying training still used today, trainee airmen being shown how to recover from difficult situations, such as spinning, from which recovery had previously been largely a matter of luck and instinct. A further improvement was the fitting of voice pipes so that communication was possible between pilot and instructor. The Training Squadrons were again under pressure as the Imperial German Air Service gained ascendancy in the air over Flanders. In April 1917 the RFC lost 131 aircraft, a third of its strength in France, and 316 airmen, a third of those involved. Not for nothing was this period known as 'Bloody April'. The arrival of the SE5, Sopwith Camel, and French Spad VII once more swung the air war in the Allies' favour, and so the Training Squadrons could again concentrate on turning out pilots with training which helped them to survive the air fighting, whereas in the spring pilots were so desperately needed that they were sent to France with very little flying experience, falling easy prey to the German Albatross scouts. The next period of excessive losses came when the RFC was thrown piecemeal into the battle to stop the German offensive of March 1918.

A further reorganisation in the training structure came in the summer of 1918 when the flying training establishments were redesignated Training Depot Stations (TDS). The purpose of these was to speed up the training process by housing squadrons which would train pilots on aircraft like the Avro, and then teach them to fly operational aircraft as these were delivered to the squadron. When the pilots were proficient the instructors and newly qualified pilots moved, with their aircraft, to an operational airfield ready for the fray — being replaced by a further supply of new pilots. The TDS thus had something of the same role as today's Flying Training Schools and Operational Conversion Units combined. The Training Depot Stations in Lincolnshire were 34 TDS Scampton, 39 TDS Spitalgate, 40 TDS Harlaxton, 46 TDS at South Carlton and 48 TDS at Waddington. In addition 59 TDS formed at Scopwick (later called Digby) in September 1918.

On 1 April 1918 the Royal Air Force was formed by the amalgamation of the RFC and RNAS and further TDS were formed from the RNAS training station at Cranwell. These were initially numbered 201, 202 and 213 TDS, but were soon renumbered to bring them into line with the other TDS, 201 becoming 56 TDS, 202 - 57 and 213 - 58. Cranwell also had a wireless operator school, and its armament training school at Freiston became the RAFs 4 School of Aerial Fighting, later 4 Fighting School, responsible for training scout pilots in gunnery. At Harpswell 199 Sdn was established to train pilots and observers for night operations which were now being flown by Independent Force RAF over Germany. 199 Sdn was disbanded in June 1919.

5 *RE 7, probably of 44 Reserve Sdn, at Harlaxton in 1917, when many of the personnel were Australian.* (C Schnabel, via John Walls).

Training did have its lighter moments, young pilots being rather foolhardy; at Scampton it is recorded that a favourite trick after take-off was to disappear down the Cliff, thus bringing the crash tender along at full speed. Several airmen already famous, or later to become so, served at the Lincolnshire training airfields. 11 Training Sdn at Scampton was commanded by Capt Robert Saundby, deputy to Harris at Bomber Command HQ in World War II. 24 Training Wing at Grantham was commanded by Lt Col Charles Portal, Chief of the Air Staff in World War II, who married Joan Welby, of Denton Manor, at Grantham Church in July 1919. 23 Training Wing at South Carlton, which was responsible for 34 and 46 TDS was, in early 1918, commanded by Lt Col Louis Strange, who earlier gained fame when he was thrown from the cockpit of his spinning Martinsyde over France, hung on to his Lewis gun, which was mounted on the top wing, and managed to tip the aircraft right way up and land back in the cockpit. Col Strange had this to say about training in his Wing.

'There were not enough pupils or instructors to make good use of the total number of machines on the establishment and yet there were so many machines under repair that we were continually up against a shortage. The workshops were well organised and well run but they had too many jobs to cope with. The instructors too were hopelessly overworked and I said we must have more of them [Strange soon changed matters] . . . . with the result that we made a mighty effort to meet the monthly demand for pilots for overseas

work and at the same time keep back a number of promising pupils as future instructors.

Work in a Training Wing was no joke. The write-off of one machine for every 140 hours flying meant the loss of something between thirty and forty machines a month, in addition to some seventy or eighty minor crashes. In May of 1918 for instance, we had sixteen fatal accidents in the 23rd Wing . . . . but the work had to go on at a still more feverish pace in order to cope with the overseas requirements, for at that time the monthly output of pilots from Home Establishment was well in the neighbourhood of 400.

There was, however, a lighter side to our strenuous days at Lincoln. The keen competition between ourselves and the neighbouring Wings gave us many opportunities of letting off steam . . . . Early one morning Waddington turned out to find a few nice healthy young ash saplings flourishing on their aerodrome, the implication being, of course, that they grew there because the aerodrome was never used'.

(Strange L *Recollections of an airman* John Hamilton 1933).

6   *South Carlton, home of 39, 45 and 61 Training Sdns, in March 1918, shows a typical WWI airfield layout. Ermine Street runs across the top right corner with Hallifirs wood in the foreground.* (Lincolnshire Library Service).

The typical World War I training airfield was a grass square with 2,000 foot sides. It had three pairs of hangars (of brick or wood), plus one single, all 180ft x 100ft, and up to twelve canvas Bessoneaux hangars. Aircraft of this period were still wood framed and fabric covered and were thus very susceptible to weather damage, hence the large number of hangars. Living quarters, stores, offices etc were all wooden huts. Some first war hangars can still be seen at Cranwell and until 1975 another example stood at South Carlton, where some original huts still survive.

The loss of pilots was not the only replacement problem facing the RFC; for every pilot killed or wounded there was an aeroplane written off or badly damaged. Here again Lincolnshire played a large part as Lincoln was, during World War I, one of the largest aircraft manufacturing areas in the world. The full story of this effort is told by John Walls in his excellent series of three booklets, so it is sufficient to say that three Lincoln firms were engaged in the industry, Ruston Proctor, Robey and Clayton & Shuttleworth. To receive these aircraft into service, the RFC established 4 Aircraft Acceptance Park on West Common, Lincoln. It was to here that the manufacturers delivered their aircraft where they were tested and any Service modifications incorporated. If deemed satisfactory they were then collected by RFC or RNAS pilots and flown back to their squadrons. Flt Sub-Lt Rochford again —

'On Boxing Day [1917] Harold Ireland and I went to London by train on our way to Lincoln where we were to collect two Sopwith Camels, built by Clayton & Shuttleworth, from the Acceptance Park. These we were to deliver to RNAS Dover. We stayed overnight in London and the following morning continued our journey by train to Lincoln and arrived at the Acceptance Park in time for some lunch. Afterwards we collected our Camels and took off. We had no maps and knowing the compasses in our machines were far from accurate we decided to follow the railway line towards London'.

Rochford later picked the wrong line out of Peterborough and became lost, an incident which illustrates the navigation methods still being used at that time. 4AAP moved to Bracebridge Heath after the war and the sheds which had been erected on the Common were soon dismantled. Its stay at Bracebridge Heath was short, the unit disbanding in 1920. Bracebridge was also briefly the home of 120 Sdn, recently returned from France. A further back-up RFC unit in Lincoln was 6 (Lincoln) Stores Depot Park, on Longdales Road, which housed large quantities of aircraft spares and other equipment for the surrounding airfields.

Royal Air Force — Anti-submarine patrols

Although Killingholme's flying boats and those of the other seaplane stations patrolled against U-boats, they covered the sea away from the coast, and the U-boats were becoming a menace in coastal waters, especially on the north east coast. Accordingly, in April 1918, the RAF decided to patrol the coastal shipping lanes at 20 minute intervals from land bases, and the aircraft chosen was the DH6, many of which were surplus to training requirements. Although the single seater version could carry bombs an observer's weight displaced these but despite the unsuitability of the aircraft for offensive action the tactics were a great success, only two vessels being attacked whilst under DH6 escort. New squadrons were formed, each with three or four dispersed flights, and not unexpectedly a flight was allocated to patrol the Humber estuary. 251 Sdn formed at Seaton Carew, Co. Durham, in April 1918, and one of its flights came to a new airfield at Greenland Top near Keelby. This flight was later given the identity of 505 Flight 251 Sdn and its DH6s continued these patrols until the Squadron disbanded in early 1919. 505 Flight was joined in its patrols in 1918 by 404 Flight of 248 Sdn whose HQ was at Hornsea. This Flight moved into another new station at North Coates Fitties, where it flew Short 225 and Sopwith Baby seaplanes until disbanded in March 1919. All anti-sub operations in the area came under the control of 18 (Operations) Group, RAF, whose HQ was at Habrough (possibly Habrough Grange?).

Thus, Lincolnshire's part in World War I in the air came to an end. Mainly a training area, the county had performed a vital if unglamorous role. Killingholme, Greenland Top and North Coates had helped to keep the submarines away from our convoys, while the HD Sdns had defeated the once dreaded Zeppelins.

Part Two

Between the Wars

The war weary British people celebrated the end of the 'war to end wars' and the majority of airmen looked forward to 'demob'. Squadrons flew back from France to disband, some of them to the Lincolnshire airfields. Most of the TDS also disbanded, as did the HD Squadrons, and by 1920 only Cranwell, Scopwick and Spitalgate remained as active airfields. Most of the other airfields quickly reverted to farmland.

The RAF College

The infant RAF was the subject of covetous glances from Generals and Admirals anxious to regain control of their respective air arms. Trenchard was reappointed Chief of the Air Staff, having resigned during 1918 because of disagreements with the government, and it was largely due to his organisation and foresight that the threatened takeover was averted. For example, the Generals and Admirals suggested that RAF officers should be trained at Army and Navy Colleges, after which they would have flying training with the Air Force. It was also suggested that the RAF should use the other Services' medical, dental, engineering and other facilities. Trenchard realized that the RAF must have its own tradition to survive and was faced with the choice, because of limited finance, between establishing a firm training foundation and few operational squadrons, or adopting the 'sharing' suggestion and having more squadrons. Trenchard chose the former course and the first step was the foundation of an RAF College on the lines of Dartmouth and Sandhurst, through which would pass the cadets destined for permanent commissions in the RAF. The site chosen for this College was Cranwell,

> *'an ideal place for the purpose, with a large and excellent aerodrome and perfect flying surroundings'.*

17

Thus spake Trenchard, but he also had a further motive — Cranwell was well away from the bright lights likely to distract these young men from their studies.

'Marooned in the wilderness, cut off from pastimes they couldn't organise for themselves, they would find life cheaper, healthier and more wholesome'.

Career other ranks were to enter the Service through Halton, the technical training school. As Trenchard put it

'I have laid the foundations of a castle. If nobody builds anything bigger than a cottage on them, it will at least be a very good cottage'.

The first cadets course began on 5 February 1920 under the command of Air Commodore C A H Longcroft. The aircraft were Avro 504Ks, with advanced training on DH9s, Bristol F2Bs, Snipes or Vimys, depending on the pupil aptitude. Apart from flying there was great emphasis on ground training and the complete course lasted for two years. Until Halton was ready for occupation in 1926 the first apprentices also trained at Cranwell, and one of these was Frank Whittle, jet engine pioneer. His abilities as an engineer were obviously recognised by the instructors, for at the end of his three year apprenticeship he was one of five awarded a cadetship to the College, in 1926.

7   *The Motor Transport section at Cranwell in 1919. The vehicles are mainly Leylands and Ford Model Ts, and some WRAF drivers can be seen.* (Lincolnshire Library Service).

In addition to the mechanical apprentices 1 Electrical and Wireless School was stationed at Cranwell and there was an RAF Hospital to serve the airfields in the area. The RAF Cadet College, as it was known until January 1929, created great interest among foreign visitors as it was the first college to train officers for permanent commissions in an air force. Flying took place from the South Aerodrome and in 1923 the aircraft line up was A Flight — Avro 504Ks (white wheels), B Flight — F2Bs (blue wheels), C Flight — Avro 504Ks (red wheels), D Flight — F2Bs (black/white quartered wheels). Each aircraft carried its flight letter and aircraft number on its engine cowling. Apart from flying there were also many other things to be learnt, including the workings of the internal combustion engine; to encourage interest in this subject each cadet was issued with a war surplus P & M motorbike, which he was expected to keep in working order and was issued with free petrol and oil for this purpose. This practice ceased when the press publicised it as 'wasteful expenditure', which perhaps did the RAF a favour, as there were more Cadets injured motor cycling than there were flying! T E Lawrence (of Arabia) joined the RAF after World War I under the pseudonym of A/C Ross but was discharged later and then joined the Royal Tank Corps. However the RAF held more appeal for him and on 24 August 1925, as AC2 Shaw, he arrived at Cranwell posted to B Flight. In his book on his RAF life Lawrence recalls his days at Cranwell with obvious affection — for example

> 'our hanger shelters a calm crescent of tarmac and grass and its open mouth is a veritable suntrap. Through the afternoon eight of us lay there waiting for a kite which had gone away south . . . and was overdue. Wonderful, to have it for our duty to do nothing but wait hour after hour in the warm sunshine, looking out southward'.

On another occasion Lawrence describes how, on his motorbike, he raced a Bristol Fighter

> 'from Whitewash Villas, our neighbour aerodrome [presumably Digby] along the Sleaford-Lincoln road. An approaching car pulled nearly into the ditch at the sight of our race. The Bif was zooming among the trees and telegraph poles, with my scurrying spot only eight yards ahead . . . . A long mile before the first houses I closed down and coasted to the crossroads by the hospital. Bif caught up, banked, climbed and turned for home, waving to me for as long as he was in sight'.
>
> (Lawrence TE *The Mint* Cape 1955 by permission of A W Lawrence.)

Flying was a more carefree occupation in those days! By the early 1930s the Junior Term flew Avro 504Ns, the Senior Term having Siskins for those cadets destined for fighters and Atlases for the prospective bomber

8   *De Havilland DH 9A, J 7317, of B Flight, RAF Cadet College, 1925. It has been converted into a two-seat trainer, and behind it can be seen a Bristol F2b. (P H T Green).*

pilots. Siskins were notoriously difficult to land, causing several accidents and it was recorded that *'a Siskin lip and a bloody nose were regarded as honourable scars'*. In fact accidents were still fairly common, 56 RAF aircrew being killed in 1930, six of these at Cranwell; though from 1920-30 there were only 8 fatalities at Cranwell in 45,000 flying hours.

The South Airfield was very large by the standards of the day and was used as the starting point of the RAF Long Distance Flights, the long take off run being necessary for these fuel laden aircraft. May 1927 saw a modified Hawker Horsley, piloted by Flt Lt C R Carr with Flt Lt Gillman as navigator, leave for a non-stop flight to India, but it was forced down in the Persian Gulf after flying 3,420 miles. After this failure the Air Ministry purchased two Fairey Long-Range Monoplanes. The first, crewed by Sdn Ldr Jones-Williams and Flt Lt Jenkins, left Cranwell on 24 April 1929 and landed at Karachi on 26 April having flown non stop in 50 hours 37 minutes. This aircraft crashed later in the year on a flight to South Africa. The second aircraft piloted by Sdn Ldr Gayford with Flt Lt Nicholetts as navigator finally gained the World long-distance record for Britain, leaving Cranwell on 6 February 1933 and arriving at Walvis Bay, South Africa on the 8th — 5,309 miles in 57 hours 25 minutes. France broke this record in August the same year, but three Vickers Wellesleys regained it for Britain in November 1938 when, having left Cranwell for Ismailia, Egypt, they flew non stop from Ismailia to Darwin, Australia — 7,162 miles in 48 hours. Other interesting events were the building of the Cranwell series of light aircraft designed by Flt Lt Comper and built by the Cranwell Light Aeroplane Club to take part in the Lympne Light Aircraft Trials. An entry for the 1925 Schneider

Trophy race was tested at Cranwell, the Napier Gloster flown by Mr Carter. Unfortunately the undercarriage hit the ground and the machine crashed, seriously injuring the pilot.

Training was Cranwell's real purpose and this carried on unabated — congestion at the main airfield meant that large fields in the neighbourhood were used as 'forced landing grounds' and two of these were at Temple Bruer and Wellingore. In 1934 several changes took place. The new College building, designed by James West, was officially opened by the Prince of Wales on 11 October 1934. It was, and is, an impressive building, much more befitting its role than the old World War I huts it partially replaced. The revolving light installed in the tower flashed white every three seconds and was visible for 20 miles on a clear night. More modern aircraft also arrived, Avro Tutors replacing the ageing 504s, Bulldogs the Siskins, and Harts the Atlases. The RAF expansion also brought new units to Cranwell; the School of Store Accounting and Storekeeping in 1934, (becoming the Equipment Training School in 1936) a Supplies Depot in 1936, HQ 21 Group, Training Command, 1938, and

9 *Single and two-seat Armstrong-Whitworth Siskins at Cranwell in the early 1930s.* (RAF Cranwell, via P H T Green).

the School of Clerks Accounting in 1939. The Empire Air Day of 1937 gave Cranwell a chance to show the Lincolnshire public what the RAF could do. 9,000 people visited the station and saw a flying programme opened by a formation of nine Harts and nine Tutors. Then came a message pick-up by an Audax, crazy flying by two Tutors, aerobatics by two Furies (which had replaced the Bulldogs), bombing by a Wallace, a flypast by three Valentias of the Electrical and Wireless School, bombing by three Harts, attack on a towed target by a Fury, and a massed flypast by 21 aircraft. In addition, the new Blenheim I and Anson showed off their paces. A similar display at Waddington was marred by the fatal crash of an aircraft from 2FTS Digby.

10 *Cranwell trained pilots of the Commonwealth Air Forces as well as those of the RAF. This group are the first six pilots of the Royal Indian Air Force which was formed in 1933.* (RAF Cranwell, via P H T Green).

The Flying Training Schools

Having discovered the county's suitability for flying training the RAF decided, after World War I, that all the criteria still applied and so established two of its six newly titled Flying Training Schools here, No 3 at Scopwick and No 6 at Spitalgate. The two schools were short lived in these locations. 3 FTS moving to Spitalgate in April 1922, while 6, which had never received aircraft, moved to Manston in May 1921. Spitalgate quickly grew into a large station as, in addition to 3 FTS, two day bomber squadrons also arrived, 39 Sdn in February 1921 and 100 Sdn in February 1922. Both were equipped with the De Havilland 9A, the RAFs maid of all work in those early post war years. 100 Sdn re-equipped with Fairey Fawns before leaving for Eastchurch in August 1924 and 39 Sdn departed in January 1928, leaving the station solely to 3 FTS which continued training pilots for the RAFs many peace time tasks. Scopwick, now called Digby to avoid confusion with RAF Shotwick, Cheshire, (which to make doubly certain, was renamed Sealand), had a short period of what was to become known as 'Care and Maintenance' and then received another FTS to replace No 3. This was 2 FTS which arrived from Duxford in June 1924 and continued with similar duties to 3FTS. It is interesting to note that by 1925 the Services Flying Training Schools were 1 Netheravon, Wilts, 2 Digby, 3 Spitalgate, 4 Abu Sueir, Egypt (for pilots destined for service in the Middle East) and 5 at Sealand, Cheshire, again emphasising the suitability of Lincolnshire for flying training. At this time, any potential enemy (France was considered the only danger) would be on the continent, and the operational squadrons were mainly based in southern Britain, so as to be in range of Europe. It was not until the resurgence of Germany as a military power, plus longer ranged aircraft designs, that Lincolnshire began to move into the RAFs front line.

Numbers 2 and 3 Flying Training Schools received two types of students, University entrants with permanent commissions, and recruits seeking Short Service commissions. (The third type of entry was via Cranwell). Aircraft used for training were the ubiquitous Avro 504Ks, later replaced by 504Ns, — the Lynx-Avro (so called because of its change to the Armstrong-Siddeley Lynx engines), Sopwith Snipes, Bristol F2Bs, Siskins, DH9s and Vickers Vimys, and later Armstrong-Whitworth Atlases. Several officers later to gain high rank served at Digby in the 1920s. W/C Tedder, later Marshall of the RAF Lord Tedder, was CO (the station school is now named after him), and among the instructors was Flt Lt F J Fogarty (later ACM Sir Francis Fogarty), and F/O F Whittle (last heard of at Cranwell), F/O Whittle was chosen to take part in the popular 'crazy flying' event at the RAF pageant Hendon, the idea being

11 *Hawker Hart Trainers of 2 FTS in the hangar at Digby, mid 1930s.* (John Walls).

for two pilots to fly as though it were their first time in an aircraft. During the rehearsals at Digby Whittle was involved in two crashes, luckily escaping serious injury in both. However, after the second one

> *'I was met by a furious Flight Commander who, his face flushed with rage, sarcastically demanded "Why don't you take all my bloody aeroplanes into the middle of the aerodrome and set fire to them — its quicker!"'*

(Whittle later received congratulations on his performance at Hendon from the AOC 23 Group). 2 FTS began to run down during the early 1930s and eventually closed in December 1933).

Meanwhile 3FTS continued to operate in much the same way as Digby, equipped with similar types of aircraft, with the addition of the Hawker Tomtit and Bristol Bulldog trainer. The RAF expansion scheme began to come into effect and a change in the training pattern took place to cope with the much larger intake of trainee pilots: initial training was undertaken at civilian manned Elementary and Reserve Flying Training Schools (ERFTS), on Tiger Moths, Blackburn B2s and later, Miles Magisters. One of these Schools was formed at Grimsby in June 1938, operated by the Herts & Essex Aero Club, but disbanded when World War II started. Pilots learnt the basics of flying there and then came to the RAF FTS for advanced flying and instruction in Service matters. The course lasted for a very busy year. At Grantham — as Spitalgate was now

24

known — in the mid thirties, there were fifteen flying instructors plus ground instructors, and a typical day for the students started with PT and drill, then carried on with flying instruction and lectures on admin, navigation, armament, engines, discipline, meteorology, RAF history and organisation, rigging, wireless and aeronautical theory. Flying instruction included four cross-country flights to a point not less than 60 miles away, one of which was Sealand; sport was also an important activity. At the end of the year's course pilots were awarded their 'Wings' and posted to their squadrons for operational training. The aircraft used by this time was the Hawker Hart Trainer, with the Hawker Fury for advanced armament and aerobatics training. 2FTS, which re-opened in October 1934 due to the demand for pilots generated by the RAFs expansion, was now commanded by Gp Capt T Leigh-Mallory (later ACM Sir Trafford Leigh-Mallory), while a star of the station rugger team was Flt Lt George Beamish, who became an Air Marshal.

By 1937 the RAFs expansion scheme was taking effect and the threat was plain for all to see — Hitler's Germany across the North Sea. Lincolnshire was therefore in the front line and airfields were needed for operational squadrons. Consequently 3 FTS moved to a new airfield at South Cerney in Gloucestershire, and 2 FTS, a month later, followed it south to Brize Norton, Oxon. Flying training was not finished in the county however, because after a brief spell of just over a year as a bomber station Grantham returned to training with the formation of 12 FTS in October 1938. This was one of four new FTS opened during 1938 to cope with the continuing expansion of the RAF and the consequent

12 *Hawker Hind Trainers (centre) and Miles Magisters of 25 ERFTS at Waltham aerodrome, Grimsby, c1938.* (Humberside Libraries, via P H T Green).

need for pilots. Students arrived from ERFTS for a 22 week course aimed at raising them to operational flying standards — note the reduction from the one year course of 3 FTS. The expansion of flying training not only required new schools, airfields and instructors, but also aircraft. The British aircraft industry was concentrating on fighters and bombers and the only advanced single engined trainer being produced was the Miles Master. The Air Ministry therefore sent a Purchasing Commission to the USA and there they ordered Lockheed Hudson patrol bombers, and trainers, chief of which was the North American Harvard. The Harvard was an ideal aircraft for training pilots destined for fighter squadrons as it had such refinements as retractable undercarriage and flaps and a fair performance. It served with the RAF until 1953 and Grantham gained a significant niche in the Service's history, being the first unit since World War I to use American aircraft and the first to operate the Harvard. The residents of Grantham and surrounds were soon made aware of this as the Harvard was notorious for its raucous engine sound. However, this was not to last long, as a change to twin-engine training saw the Harvards replaced by Ansons before the war.

The three large flying training establishments in Lincolnshire were aimed at turning out pilots who were also trained in navigation, there being no navigators as such in the RAF in the 1920s and early 1930s. Air gunners were squadron groundcrew who volunteered for flying. Armament training was required for these and once more Lincolnshire's geographical features made it the RAFs choice — this time for the mudflats of the Wash and the large sandy beaches of the East Coast. The RAF needed somewhere it could drop bombs and fire machine guns at targets, which of course needed to be done without risk to civilians. In 1926-27 three armament practice camps were opened at Catfoss in the East Riding, North Coates Fitties and Sutton Bridge in Lincolnshire; to these three camps, each year, came all home based squadrons of the RAF and Fleet Air Arm for bombing and gunnery training. The range for North Coates was on the sands at Donna Nook and that for Sutton Bridge on the mud near Holbeach St Matthew. At Donna Nook, in the early thirties, were three bombing targets, one of which could be illuminated at night, and ten gunnery targets. Two squadrons were detached at any one time to North Coates for approximately a month and there was a Station Flight of Fairey Gordons, which towed drogue targets for air-to-air gunnery. These APCs were open only during the summer months — Sutton Bridge for example generally operated from March to October/November, and was not officially placed on a permanent basis until March 1936.

By 1937 it was becoming evident that the new generation of RAF aircraft would require specialised aircrew other than pilots and the Observer's

13 *A Fairey Gordon flying over Donna Nook range, with the gunner firing at the targets, c 1934.* (Flight International).

14 *Westland Wallaces of North Coates Station Flight flying over the Lincolnshire coast. 1936. Nearest the camera is K 6045.* (C S Warr).

flying badge, last seen in the Great War, was reintroduced. Since 1934 groundcrew airmen had received observer training to qualify them for part time flying duties and an Air Observer School (AOS) opened at North Coates in January 1936, where a two month course on bombing and gunnery was undertaken alongside the activities of 2 Armament Training School (ATS), the new title of the APC. 2 ATS and the AOS merged in 1937 to become 2 Air Armament School (AAS), and this in turn became 1 AOS in March and left for North Wales on the outbreak of war. Sutton Bridge, which became 3 ATS, also moved to safer territory in September 1939. A third Lincolnshire station heavily involved in armament training was Manby which opened in August 1938 as 1 AAS; it ran courses for armament officers, air gunners, bomb aimers, armourers and instructors, with a variety of aircraft — Battles, Wallaces, Hinds and Furies. The bombing and gunnery range at Theddlethorpe, opened in 1935, was taken over by Manby. The station was getting into its stride by September 1939 and unlike North Coates and Sutton Bridge, 1 AAS remained in situ.

15 *A Fairey Fawn light bomber of 503 Sdn, the first type with which it was equipped.* (John Walls).

16 *A Handley-Page Hinaidi of 503 (County of Lincoln) Sdn, c1930.* (John Walls).

Operational Flying

In 1925, in an attempt to strengthen the RAF, the Auxiliary Air Force (AuxAF) was formed to support the regular squadrons. The Aux AF squadrons were based near large centres of population and were initially light bomber units. Alongside the Aux AF squadrons were formed the Special Reserve Squadrons. These differed from the Auxiliaries which were manned largely by civilian volunteers as the Reserve or Cadre Squadrons had one complete flight composed of regular officers and airmen, the other flight or flights being manned by Special Reserve airmen. The squadron CO was also a regular officer, again unlike the Auxiliary Squadrons. Thus the Cadre squadrons were much more Regular Air Force then part time volunteer, although officially reserve units and were distinguished by being numbered in the 500 series, while the Auxiliary Squadrons were in the 600 range. The second Cadre unit to form was 503 Squadron and to house it, Waddington (which had retained its buildings and airfield unlike most of the other World War I stations), was reopened in 1926. 503 Sdn aircraft were Fairey Fawn light bombers, but it became a night bomber unit when re-equipped with Handley Page Hyderabads in 1929, a role which foreshadowed Waddington's later use. Hinaidis retained the Handley Page connection until 1935 when the

Squadron resumed a day bomber role with Westland Wallaces and, a year later, Hawker Harts. 503s first CO was Wing Cdr The Hon. Twistleton-Wykeham-Fiennes, and in April 1929 the Squadron was officially named 503 'County of Lincoln' Squadron. Practice bombing was carried out over the airfield, the target being a chalk circle, and 8½ and 11½lb smoke bombs were used, the impact being plotted by two quadrants on the ground. 503 had few accidents and only two fatal crashes are recorded.

17 *Fatal crash on Saturday afternoon, 6 February 1937. Hawker Hart, K 3025, of 503 Sdn, flown by P/O Forte with air gunner LAC East, in a ploughed field near Waddington. The fuselage was sawn around the pilot's cockpit and the tail pulled down to get the pilot from the wreckage. Note Waddington's present hangars under construction in the background. (Harold Willars).*

In May 1937 the Squadron was joined by two new units of the rapidly growing Bomber Command, which had been formed on 14 July 1936 under a restructuring of the RAF. These new squadrons were initially equipped with interim bomber types until the new bombers came into service. 50 and 110 Sdns had the Hawker Hind, but a month after their formation two further squadrons formed, 44 Sdn and 88 Sdn, also with

Hinds, 88 staying only a month before leaving for Boscombe Down, Wiltshire. 44 was the first Waddington squadron to receive new equipment when its Blenheim Is arrived in December, but the other three squadrons entered 1938 with the Hind biplane. 110 soon got its Blenheims, leaving 503 and 50 feeling rather envious of their companion units. The Blenheim was a twin engined monoplane with enclosed crew positions, gun turret, and a maximum speed of 210mph. The Hind, on the other hand, was little changed from the World War I bombers — a single engined biplane with open cockpits, the rear one with a Lewis gun, and a speed of 186mph. If war had come with the Munich crisis of 1938 many RAF squadrons would have flown into battle with out-of-date aircraft like this. 503 never attracted as many reserve airmen as had been hoped and 1 November 1938 was a sad day for the personnel when the squadron disbanded, never to be reformed, although its airmen could transfer to its successor unit 616 (South Yorkshire) Sdn Aux AF, at Doncaster.

Waddington was now an all Regular, three-squadron station and it remained like this until, under a type rationalisation, 110 Sdn Blenheims moved down to Wattisham, Suffolk, to join other Blenheim squadrons in East Anglia. 50 and 44 Sdns both re-equipped with Handley Page Hampdens, a type which was to play a large part in early operations from Lincolnshire bases, and both squadrons were at Waddington when World War II broke out. In the meantime RAF expansion meant that further airfields were needed in eastern England and it was natural for World War I sites to be examined for suitability. Scampton was selected and work began in 1935. There was some local resistance to this, a workman's hut being burnt down, but by October 1936 the airfield was ready and 9 and 214 Sdns arrived, both night bomber units and equipped respectively with the Heyford and the Virginia biplanes. Much of the accommodation was still under construction so tents were in evidence for the first months. The Ginny as the Virginia was affectionately known, was obsolescent, and in January 214 re-equipped with the Harrow, another interim type, but at least a monoplane. This type did not see much service in Lincolnshire as 214 moved to Norfolk to be replaced, in June, by the reformed 148 Sdn with the Audax, another elderly biplane, soon to be exchanged for a modern type, the Vickers Wellesley. When 148 and 9 left Scampton in March the two new squadrons, 49 and 83, were both Hind equipped but by September 1939 both were operating Hampdens. Hemswell was the third new station, again built on a World War I site, and its squadrons arrived in early 1937, 144 and 61 Sdns having Audaxes and Ansons until the autumn, when 144 got its new Blenheims, followed by 61 in early 1938. However the Hampden had been chosen as the type to be operated from Lincolnshire, and the

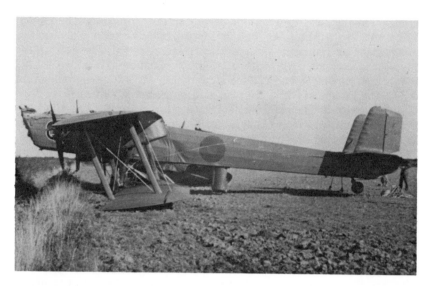

18 *A rather bent Handley-Page Heyford, K 3498, of 99 Sdn, which force-landed at Donna Nook in 1934, while on armament practice camp.* (W/Cdr S Threapleton, via P H T Green).

Hemswell squadrons re-equipped with these in 1939. Grantham, having lost 3 FTS, also became a bomber station, briefly housing 113 and 211 Sdns with Hinds. During 1938 these two units were replaced by two Battle squadrons, 106 and 185, but these left in October 1938 and the station reverted to a training role, presumably because of its limited size. The Lincolnshire bomber stations were controlled by 5 Group HQ, Bomber Command. Initially located at Mildenhall, it soon moved to its operational area when in October 1937 the Air Ministry took over a large house at the foot of Spitalgate Hill, Grantham, called 'St Vincents'. On the outbreak of war 5 Group was commanded by AV-M A T Harris. One of its Air Weapons Ranges was at Wainfleet, opened in August 1938 on the site of an Artillery Range used in the 1890s, and the other was at Holbeach.

The fact that Lincolnshire was a part of England nearest to Germany and suitable for mounting a bombing offensive against that country worked also in reverse. It was in reach of German bombers which would strike at the bomber airfields and also cross the county on their way to the industrial areas of the North Midlands, South Yorkshire and Lancashire. To counter this threat Fighter Command also moved into Lincolnshire, 12 Group establishing two squadrons at Digby in November 1937. Like the bomber squadrons, their aircraft were elderly, 46 having Gauntlets and 73 Gladiators, both biplanes. These aircraft, doped silver, carried the colourful markings of the between-the-war fighter squadrons, 46 having a red arrowhead on the fuselage, while 73 had a blue and yellow flash. The Munich crisis saw these markings disappear and when the two squadrons got Hurricanes in 1938 they were in earth and dark green camouflage.

The airfields opened between 1935 and 1940, planned under the expansion scheme, were quite attractive. Buildings were of brick and built to a set design so that each station appeared very similar. The designs were approved by the Royal Fine Arts Commission and the Society for the Preservation of Rural England was asked for its views. The typical station of this period had a grass airfield with three large hangars which dwarfed the other buildings. Barrack blocks were two storey, and married quarters were provided for officers and airmen, with large messes for junior ranks, senior NCOs and officers. Older airfields were usually (but not always) brought up to this standard and examples are Waddington, Scampton, Digby, Hemswell, Manby and Kirton-in-Lindsey.

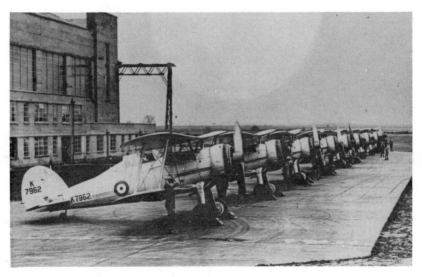

19 *Gloster Gladiators of 73 Sdn at Digby in 1938.* (RAF Cranwell, via P H T Green).

20 *A 'vic' of Handley-Page Hampdens over the Cathedral c1939.* (John Walls).

Part Three

World War II — the early years 1939-1942

Guy Gibson, later to become Lincolnshire's best known airman, was on leave in Wales in late August 1939. On the 31st he received a telegram which simply said 'Return to Unit immediately'. Gibson was at that time a F/O with 83 Sdn at Scampton:

> *'Sunny Scampton we call it because it's in Lincolnshire and one doesn't see much sun up there [and when he arrived back at the camp] . . . . complete bedlam reigned . . . . There were tractors driving round the perimeter roads in the sweltering heat, some with long bomb trailers bouncing along behind; others pulling our Hampdens along cinder tracks far into the country to dispersal points fairly safe from enemy bombs. All round the airfield sand-bagged gun emplacements were being put up by aerodrome defence squads, but there were not many guns. Gas officers were running round placing yellow detectors in the right places'.*
>
> (Gibson G *Enemy coast ahead* Michael Joseph, 1946).

This scene was being repeated at Waddington and Hemswell, while similar activities took place at Digby, Cranwell, Grantham, Manby, North Coates and Sutton Bridge. This preparation was not to be wasted, as on 3 September Prime Minister Chamberlain told the country that we were at war with Germany. Almost immediately the Lincolnshire bases mounted their first operations; at Waddington 44 Sdn sent 9 Hampdens on armed reconnaissance over Heligoland Roads; while at Scampton 49 sent 3 aircraft on armed reconnaissance over the North Sea, with 5 aircraft of 83 Sdn. (Guy Gibson recorded that the pilots had never taken off with a full bomb load before!). No enemy ships were seen and the aircraft brought their bombs back. 144 Sdn flew its first 'op' on 26 September, again an armed 'recce' and again with no result, but became the first squadron to drop its bombs in anger, when on the 29 September, three Hampdens bombed two German destroyers in the Heligoland Bight. Such was the fear that German bombers would destroy our aircraft on the ground that the six Lincolnshire squadrons were withdrawn to pre-arranged 'scatter' bases, Tollerton and Newton in Nottinghamshire and several airfields in Lancashire. When the threatened attacks did not materialize the Hampdens returned home towards the end of September and continued to fly similar operations to those mentioned above for the rest of the year. 144 Sdn suffered its first casualty during an operation searching unsuccessfully for the German battleship 'Deutschland'. Bad weather dictated a diversion to Leuchars in Scotland and off the coast the formation was mistakenly attacked by Spitfires of 602 Sdn which hit two aircraft, one of which ditched killing the air gunner. Bad aircraft recognition caused many similar unnecessary incidents throughout the war.

Fighter Operations

A third Hurricane squadron had now arrived at Digby, 504 (County of Nottingham) Sdn, once a sister unit of 503 (County of Lincoln), which had transferred to the Aux AF in 1936. 46 Sdn flew the first sortie on 3 September, being ordered to intercept an approaching raid which never materialized. 73 Sdn was selected to form part of the fighter wing of the Advanced Air Striking Force which was being sent to France to provide air support for the BEF. It left Digby for Cherbourg in September, one of the departing pilots being F/O 'Cobber' Kain, a New Zealander who became the RAFs first 'ace' by shooting down 17 enemy aircraft during the Squadron's nine months in France. 504 also left in October for Essex, and the two units were replaced by 611 (West Lancashire) Sdn Aux AF, equipped with Spitfire Is, and 229 Sdn, which formed at Digby on 6 October as a long range and night fighter squadron with Blenheim IFs. 611 made Digby's first enemy contact, with a German float plane, on 21 September, but no results were obtained; on the same day 46 Sdn intercepted an attack on Hull and Immingham docks during which seven enemy aircraft were shot down. Their second success came a month later when three Heinkel He115s were shot down near a British convoy. Apart from these occasional excitements all three Digby squadrons flew convoy patrols over the North Sea. 46 Sdn moved north to Acklington from November to January 1940, when it returned to Digby, while 229 re-equipped with Hurricane Is in March 1940 and the one Spitfire and two Hurricane units continued fairly uneventful routine patrols. When Germany invaded Norway in May 1940 an Anglo/French force was sent, and 46 Sdn joined it as part of its air cover. The campaign was short and 46 embarked on the carrier HMS Glorious, actually landing its aircraft on at sea, an excellent piece of flying. Tragically it was to no avail, as the 'Glorious' was sunk by the 'Scharnhorst' and 'Gneisenau' and only two members of the squadron aboard were rescued. Some personnel on another ship returned safely to Digby, where 46 worked up to operational standard again. As is evident from the lack of action described above, Digby was regarded as a 'quiet' sector by Fighter Command. In the summer of 1940, when the Command's squadrons in Southern England began to be drawn into battles over the Channel convoys, they were rotated to quieter areas to give them a breather. 1940 therefore saw a succession of fighter squadrons staying at Digby for only a month or so — 111 Sdn Hurricanes, 222 Sdn Spitfires, 56 Sdn Hurricanes, 79 Sdn Hurricanes, 151 Sdn Hurricanes and 402 Sdn Hurricanes. The Battle of Britain largely passed Digby by — in fact, from 1 July to 31 October 1940, the period regarded as the Battle of Britain, 611 Sdn claimed 1 Dornier Do 215 (2 July) and 3 Dornier Do17 (21 August), and 151 Sdn 1 Junker Ju88 (30 September).

The end of 1940 saw three units in residence. 46 Sdn having seen action in the south was back in its ancestral home, in company with 29 Sdn a night fighter unit with Blenheim 1Fs and 402 Royal Canadian Air Force (RCAF) Sdn, with Hurricanes. 402 Sdn was the first of many Canadian units to serve at Digby, and was the second Canadian fighter squadron to form in Britain. Its officers arrived at Digby on 11 December, Hurricanes arrived on the 13th, and the squadron became operational in early 1941. On its formation it was actually known as No 2 Sdn RCAF but it was decided that all Commonwealth and Allied units would receive RAF squadron numbers to avoid confusion, and on 1 March, 2 Sdn RCAF became 402 (RCAF) Sdn, RAF. 402s Hurri's worked up to operational efficiency and in May 1941 moved to Wellingore, which had become a satellite of Digby in 1940. A month later the Canadians moved south and began to fly sweeps over France.

While at Digby, 402 had been joined by another Canadian unit, 1 Sdn RCAF, which replaced 46 when it finally left Digby in February. 1 Canadian had followed a completely different path from its sister squadron, having seen action in the south of the country during the Battle of Britain and then moved to Scotland for a 'rest'. At Digby it was renumbered 401 (RCAF) Sdn and remained until October when it flew to Biggin Hill. Digby was at this time a Sector Station, which meant its operations room controlled its own squadrons and those at Wellingore and Coleby Grange. The operations room was transferred to Blankney Hall where it would be less of a target in the event of an enemy raid on Digby, and radar information was fed to Blankney from the Chain Home radar station at Stenigot, one of the first radar stations.

Although the day fighter squadrons did not see much action the Luftwaffe had begun its night blitz, and while Hurricanes and Spitfires did occasionally operate at night, night fighting was the responsibility of the

Blenheim IFs of 29 Sdn. To 29 Sdn in October 1940 came Flt Lt Guy Gibson, late of 83 (Bomber) Sdn, posted in for Flight Commander duties.

'On the aerodrome not a soul was in sight. The aircraft were covered up and the windsock hung water-logged and motionless from one of the hangars'.

Gibson, despite his long sojourn in Lincolnshire, seemingly never appreciated the county's finer points —

'At Digby, Lincolnshire is at its worst — a vast area of flatness, spreading out towards the East Fenlands of the Wash. Hardly a tree breaks the horizon, hardly a bird sings'.

At this time 29 Sdn was converting to the new Beaufighters, one of the first units to so equip, and was operating from Wellingore which was code-named WC1. In between learning to fly the Beau Gibson got married, the couple living at the 'Lion and Royal', Navenby. The squadron became operational and in March opened its score on Beaufighters when a Junkers Ju88 was sent down by the CO near Louth. The same night Bob Braham, who finished the war as the RAFs top night fighter ace, got a Dornier Do17:

'Ross and I were scrambled and vectored towards the coast near Skegness . . . . The GCI controller directed us towards the enemy, keeping up a running commentary . . . then Ross came through over the intercom. "Contact 4,000 yards and 20 degrees above. Turn gently port". This was it. I pressed the transmitter and shouted 'Contact' to the GCI controller. [The radar observer guided Braham towards the enemy aircraft until—] Yes, there he was, a black object moving ahead of me and above, still too far to make out what sort of aircraft he was . . . . Now I could clearly make out the enemy and identified him as a Dornier . . . . I had to get in closer to make certain of this. The Dornier had just crossed the coast near Skegness and might be heading for one of the Midland cities to dump his load of destruction . . . . I eased gently back on the control column, allowing a little deflection and pressed the firing button. The four cannons roared for a second then stopped. "Damn it, they've jammed", I shouted. [Ross cleared the blockage, and Braham, who was now chasing the aircraft out to sea, got in a second burst which exploded the Dornier]. The GCI operators were as bucked as we were over our success. Back at the airfield the news had gone ahead of us and we stepped out of the aeroplane to be surrounded by air and groundcrew'.

(Braham J R D *Scramble* Muller, 1961)

The night following these two victories Gibson shot down a Heinkel He111 over the North Sea. 29 was definitely in business, but in April it was posted to West Malling in Kent. By this time the German night fighters and bombers were striking back, and as Gibson put it:

'After a while the aerodromes of Lincolnshire were in the front line. We had to change the flare path, amidst exploding bombs, on many occasions'.

During 1941 three more Canadian squadrons formed up at Digby and its satellites. 409 Sdn was the second Canadian night fighter unit, starting life on elderly Defiants in June 1941, moving next month to Coleby Grange. Like 29, it converted to Beaufighters, and the new aircraft took its toll of the crews including the life of the CO Sdn Ldr Petersen; but on 1 November a Dornier Do217 was destroyed. A quiet time followed until in March a Heinkel He111 was shot down, and during the summer several victories were claimed including five in July alone.

411 Sdn also formed in June, with 412 Sdn, both on Spitfires. After working up, these units took part in fighter sweeps over the Continent being temporarily based on airfields in the south for these operations. 411 moved to Hornchurch in November 1941 but returned to Digby for brief periods twice during 1942. 412 made the short flight to Wellingore in October where it stayed the winter, with occasional forays south for a bit of action, taking its final leave of Lincolnshire in May 1942. A 412 Sdn pilot killed during its stay in Lincolnshire was a 19 year old American, P/O John Gillespie Magee who is buried in Scopwick Burial Ground. Magee was no ace and made no great reputation as a pilot. However, he will be remembered for one of the best known flying poems of World War II:

HIGH FLIGHT

"Oh! I have slipped the surly bonds of earth
And danced the skies on laughter-silvered wings;
Sunward I've climbed, and joined the tumbling mirth
Of sun-split clouds — and done a hundred things
You have not dreamed of — wheeled and soared and swung
High in the sunlit silence. Hov'ring there
I've chased the shouting wind along, and flung
My eager craft thro' footless halls of air.

Up, up the long, delirious, burning blue
I've topped the wind-swept heights with easy grace
Where never lark, nor even eagle flew—
And while with silent, lifting mind I've trod
The high, untrespassed sanctity of space,
Put out my hand and touched the face of God".

In August Digby got its first Canadian CO Gp Capt Campbell — not surprisingly, as all three squadrons in the sector were now RCAF. However, an RAF unit did replace 411 and 412, namely 92 Sdn the highest scorer in the Battle of Britain. It was posted to Digby as non-operational and in February 1942 left a Lincolnshire winter for the warmer climes of Egypt. 609 (West Riding) Sdn which arrived in November 1941 had also gained fame during the Battle, claiming over 100 aircraft destroyed up to

21 *Symbolic of the many RAF graves in the county is that of P/O John Gillespie Magee, pilot and poet, of 412 (RCAF) Sdn, in Scopwick Burial Ground.* (Lincolnshire Library Service).

October 1940. At Digby, because of its high turnover of pilots, it was nicknamed 609 Operational Training Unit, but returned south in March shortly before re-equipping with Typhoons, which brought the squadron initial trials and tribulations before eventual fame. A tragic event during 609s stay was the loss, in a collision with another Spitfire, of the Belgian ace Jean Offenberg. Offenberg had joined the Belgian Air Force in 1939 and shot down a Dornier Do17 before his country was overrun by the Germans. After several adventures he reached England, via Algeria, and joined the RAF. Serving with 145 and 609 Sdns he scored seven victories, five probables and 6½ damaged (the ½ was shared!). 609 Sdn had had a hectic time at Biggin Hill in late 1940, and was posted to Digby. Offenberg wasn't keen —

'It was Gilroy who announced the great news: "We're being moved the day after tomorrow. The Squadron's posted to Digby". At first Offenberg hardly dared credit this because the station in question was so far away from their present scene of activity. "But Digby's in Group 12, isn't it? There won't be any fighting there. They might just as well have sent us to Australia or the Belgian Congo". [However, move they did].

Digby possessed neither the comfort or the reputation of Biggin Hill . . . . If the countryside had changed, if other squadrons like warrior tribes camped with them round the airfield, the 609 was self contained and the pilots were closer than they had ever been before . . . . So they grew used to their misfortune in the icy winds that blew in from the North Sea . . . .

Sunday, 23rd November
Mass at the camp. One Section of 609 had to escort a few coasters sailing south; we met them off the Wash, some minutes flight from base. I shall eventually believe that the War is still going on up here.

From time to time the Luftwaffe sends a few bombers into the Digby sector, but very rarely, and since the weather is against this type of exercise I shall have little chance of meeting any Nazi aircraft'.

Offenberg experienced one of the problems that was to increasingly plague pilots based in eastern England.

'Returning to our point of departure I caught sight of the flare path lights at Digby. As soon as I touched down I found to my amazement that I was on a strange airfield and that the landmarks were new to me. And yet when I called Digby they had given me permission to land. Where the hell was I? How incredibly stupid. A few moments later a British Squadron Commander explained the mystery, and laughed at my discomfiture. I was at Wellingore, five miles from my own base, and I had mistaken the two fields'.

(Offenberg J *Lonely Warrior* Souvenir Press, 1956)

For the remainder of 1942 day fighter squadrons rotated through Digby on rest periods from the succession of sweeps over Europe, or as their last UK station before an overseas posting. These included 601 (County of London) Sdn which arrived in March to train up on Spitfires after an unhappy period on Bell Airacobras, an American fighter which just did not come up to the requirements of fighter operations in NW Europe. 601 then took its Spits to Malta. 421 (RCAF) Sdn formed up with Spitfires in April, 54 Sdn stayed briefly during June before shipping out to Australia and 242 Sdn came in September to prepare for a move to Algeria. A new fighter type made its first appearance in Lincolnshire when 198 Sdn formed up on Typhoon 1s in December. One unit which was to stay at Digby for a longer period was 288 (Army Co-operation) Sdn which formed in November 1941 for the purpose of training Army and RAF Regiment anti-aircraft gunners in the area, and alternated between Digby, Wellingore and Coleby. So, in December 1942 Digby housed 198 Sdn, 288 Sdn was at Wellingore and 409 Sdn at Coleby Grange. In September Digby had become officially an RCAF station.

While Digby was the county's first fighter station, the more northerly area of its Sector was taken over by a new airfield, Kirton-in-Lindsey, which was planned pre-war and had opened in May 1940. Its role was very similar to Digby's and squadrons came from the battles in the south for a rest, to train up new pilots and to fly convoy patrols off the east coast. During 1940 came 222 Sdn, Hurri's; 65 Sdn, Spits; 253 Sdn, Hurri's; 264 Sdn, equipped with Defiants (which were easy meat for German fighters and resulted in the squadron's withdrawal from day operations); 74 Sdn, Spits; 307 (Polish) Sdn, Defiant night fighters; 616 Sdn, Spits; 71 Sdn, Hurri's; 255 Sdn, Defiant night fighters, and 85 Sdn, Hurri's. Only one kill, a Junkers Ju88, was claimed, by 616 Sdn on 16 September.

71 Sdn is perhaps worth a special mention. September 1940 had seen the influx of a number of American pilots who, though officially still neutral, had volunteered to join the RAF. These were grouped together into 71 (Eagle) Sdn at Church Fenton, Yorkshire and brought their Hurricanes to Kirton in November, the first of three all-American piloted squadrons, though the groundcrew were RAF. Its first operational patrol was on 5 February 1941, but its combat record started in April, after a move to Suffolk. On America's entry into the war the three Eagle squadrons became part of the US Army Air Force (USAAF) 4th Fighter Group.

Roger Hall, himself a Lincolnshire man, gives his impression of forming up a new squadron and of night fighters:

> *'The aerodrome to which I had been posted was in my home county of Lincolnshire . . . . The countryside round the airfield was flat and at the time I arrived was covered with snow. The squadron had been formed only a week before and, therefore, its entire complement was new, that is, they had all come from other squadrons or straight from O.T.U.'s. At all events we were new to each other. In the RAF, however, people had the habit of remaining strangers at the most an hour or so and at least ten minutes particularly if they met in the bar . . . . During the next few days the entire personnel of the squadron arrived, and we started to sort ourselves out and begin training. Our C.O. Smithy, gave us a brief lecture on what our work would entail. We would*

*be given three months training to acquire and perfect the art of night intercep-
tion and night combat after which we should go south to operate against the
German night bombers. We were to spend the first month learning to handle
the Defiant during the daylight hours so that we should accustom ourselves to
its flying characteristics . . . . We started to fly these machines the day following our arrival. The Lincolnshire countryside lay beneath a mantle of snow
and the whole panorama gave the impression of something inexpressibly bleak
and melancholy. I flew over my home cautiously for I was far from happy with
the strange aircraft. It seemed heavy and cumbersome compared to the Spitfire . . . . Above us, as we flew, was a sky laden with snow clouds with their
bases little more than four thousand feet. In these conditions, the aerodrome
was difficult to find, for roads and other landmarks were all covered with
snow. Lincoln Cathedral provided a good landmark, for it stood serenely on
the top of a fairly high hill dominating the City. There were a lot of other RAF
stations close to ours, mostly bomber stations, but all constructed to the same
set pattern, and as they all presented from the air the same configuration of
buildings it was easy to become confused. [After getting used to the Defiant,
and flying at night, 255 Sdn began its first sorties against German bombers
raiding Sheffield and Hull. Flt Lt Hall was ordered to orbit above the mouth
of the Humber.] We hurried to our machine which stood silently among the
others in the dispersal area, looking like something quite sinister in its matt-
black night camouflage . . . . I opened the throttle of the heavy machine and at
once it began to move. I steered it by the alternate application of the wheel
brakes towards the 'Chance lights' which were situated at the take-off end of
the flare path . . . . The flare path was lit only by a row of goose-neck flares at
intervals of some fifty yards or so along the whole length of the grass runway.*

*[Once airborne, Hall and his gunner had orbited for half an hour when —] I
caught sight, from the corner of my eye, of a Heinkel 111 gliding silently and
apparently furtively towards the coast . . . . In a fever of excitement I switched
on the 'intercom' and shouted to Fitz "There it is Fitz — below us — see it?"
and switched over to receive. Fitz said "No — haven't seen anything yet".
While I was speaking to him I put the aircraft into a steep dive towards the
Heinkel, for I was afraid I was going to lose sight of it in the darkness . . . .
Our aircraft shuddered slightly as Fitz opened up on the bomber with the four
turret guns pointing directly backwards and firing up at the bomber's cockpit
from a range of little more than twenty yards. I looked over my shoulder as he
fired and saw the great Heinkel sitting gracefully like a bird of prey above us as
though quite stationary. I could see our bullets hitting the centre section from
underneath and the shots were like small dancing sparks creeping forwards up
to the cockpit of the enemy machine'.*

Hall R *Clouds of Fear* Bailey Bros & Swinfen, 1975

After two more attacks the Heinkel exploded, 255 Sdn's first victory.

The year 1941 saw the departure of 616, 71 and 255, the latter to Hibaldstow, a newly opened airfield which was a satellite of Kirton and which thereafter took the night fighter role, leaving the day fighters at Kirton. 616 was replaced by 65, and 452 (Royal Australian Air Force) Sdn formed up on Spitfires in April, closely followed by the second Eagle squadron, 121, in May. 452 (RAAF) was the first Australian fighter squadron in the UK and flew convoy patrols until moving south in July, while 121 with Hurricanes performed similar duties. A Junkers Ju88 was damaged on 8 August and 121 Sdn joined the West Malling Wing for occasional sweeps. Its first aircraft destroyed was unfortunately an RAF Blenheim, and the Squadron converted to Spitfires before moving to North Weald in December. 136 Sdn formed with Hurricanes in August and Kirton became its only British base, as it spent the rest of the war, and was eventually disbanded, in the Far East. 616 and 611 Sdns, both pre-war Auxiliary units, served at Kirton into the New Year and 133 Sdn, the third and last Eagle squadron, paid a visit to its sister unit's birthplace.

1942 was a year of differing nationalities at Kirton. 486 Sdn was the first Royal New Zealand Air Force (RNZAF) Squadron to serve in Lincolnshire, 306 and 303 were Polish units and 457 was Australian. The RAF was represented by one of its most famous pre-war squadrons, 43 "The Fighting Cocks", and in June a little piece of history was made when the 1st Fighter Group USAAF, equipped with Lockheed P38 Lightnings, arrived to gain operational experience with the RAF. 457 returned to Australia from Kirton to help with air defence against the Japanese but 303 Sdn was soon in action, shooting down three Junkers Ju88s while on east coast convoy patrols. It was also detached to Redhill, Surrey for the Dieppe landings and scored nine kills for the loss of one pilot. 43 Sdn used Kirton as a stepping off base before sailing for Gibraltar and the North African landings so that December 1942 saw 303 Sdn as the sole occupant of the airfield.

Hibaldstow, having opened in May 1941, saw 255 Sdn trading its Defiants in for Beaufighters IIs, and the conversion gave rise to several accidents. Declared operational in September, the Squadron moved to Coltishall, Norfolk, being replaced by 253 with Hurricane IIs. 253 was, rather unusually, a single seater squadron which operated largely at night, working with the Turbinlite Havocs of 538 Sdn. This new night fighting tactic required the Havocs, large twin engined aircraft fitted with radar and a searchlight in the nose, to track enemy aircraft and illuminate them with the searchlight for the Hurricanes to shoot down, the Havoc itself having no room for armament. It was largely unsuccessful, due to dazzle problems and also the fact that the enemy were warned by the searchlight. It soon became apparent that Beaufighters and Mosquitoes, armed and with radar, could do the job much better. However 253 and 538 shot down a Heinkel He111 on 1 May 1942. They also got a probable and two damaged before 538 was disbanded in January 1943 and 253 went to North West Africa in November 1942. Another Turbinlite Havoc unit, 532 Sdn, moved to Hibaldstow in September 1942 and disbanded a month after 538, marking the end of Hibaldstow's operational period. Hibaldstow was the only Turbinlite station to claim any damage to the enemy.

Something of a peculiarity happened when the new airfield at Goxhill opened in June 1942. It had originally been earmarked as a 1 Group bomber station and then as a fighter airfield in Kirton-in-Lindsey Sector; in fact it became a station of the USAAF 8th Air Force. Goxhill was well away from 8th Air Force operational country in East Anglia and was used initially by newly arrived Fighter Groups to acclimatize themselves to English weather and operational flying. These Groups brought unfamiliar sights to Lincolnshire skies, the P38 Lightning and P47 Thunderbolt, as well as Spitfires in American markings. Why Goxhill was chosen by the USAAF is a mystery, but to the GIs arriving there in the winter of 1942/43, with the east wind blowing up the Humber, it must have seemed like the end of the world!

Bomber Operations

Although the five fighter airfields were playing an important part in the air war it was as bomber country that Lincolnshire was known to the RAF and public alike. At the end of 1939 Scampton, Hemswell and Waddington were sending Hampdens out largely on anti-shipping patrols, as at this stage of the war neither side was bombing 'civilian' targets. Losses were quite heavy, especially to German fighters, and by early 1940 the RAF bombers were forced to operate over enemy territory only at night, a policy which continued with minor exceptions, for the rest of the war. When France and the Low Countries were invaded targets such as railway stations and bridges were bombed by the light bombers of the Advanced Air Striking Force and the mediums of the home based squadrons. Later, during the invasion scare, docks and shipping were attacked and sea mining of harbour approaches took place. It can be seen that for the six Lincolnshire Hampden squadrons there was no 'phoney war'. The number of bomber stations in the county rose to four when Binbrook opened in June 1940, its first squadrons being two Battle equipped units, 12 and 142 which had just returned from France where these light bombers had been decimated during the air offensive against the advancing Germans. (The first VCs of World War II had been awarded, posthumously, to F/O Garland and Sgt Gray, of 12 Sdn for their bravery in pressing home an attack on a bridge over the Albert Canal.) Despite the Battle's obvious vulnerability, the fear of invasion was such that the two Squadrons took part in attacks on the Channel ports which were housing the build-up of German invasion barges. Binbrook came under the control of 1 Group, Bomber Command, and as the invasion scare receded in the autumn of 1940, 12 and 142 Sdns re-equipped with Vickers Wellingtons, the aircraft on which 1 Group was to standardize.

1 Group's second Lincolnshire station opened in August 1940 when Swinderby received 300 and 301 Squadrons RAF. Both units, in fact, were Polish manned, the county's first association with these expatriate Europeans, an association which was to last right through the war and which led to many Poles settling in Lincolnshire when their homeland was annexed by the Russians. Like the Binbrook squadrons, the Poles were equipped with the Battle and raided the invasion ports, the first raid, against Boulogne, taking place on 14 September. Wellingtons had taken over from the Battles by the end of the year and the conversion allowed a break from operations, which from 14 September to 18 October had totalled 85 sorties. Bad weather affected all five bomber airfields in early 1941 and several were attacked by the Luftwaffe during this period.

Coningsby received its first squadron in February, this being 106 with Hampdens. The Hampden had borne the brunt of all 5 Group operations for eighteen hard months and Waddington was the first station to get the Hampden replacement, the Avro Manchester. 207 Sdn, formed there on 1 November 1940, was the first Squadron to operate this twin-engined heavy bomber. The first Manchester op was on 24 February 1941, six aircraft attacking a cruiser at Brest. Although German naval ships continued to attract the attention of Bomber Command the targets were increasingly becoming German cities and industry, partly in retaliation for the 'Blitz', partly because the accuracy of navigation and bombing at that time demanded large targets. 207s initial delight at getting the new bomber must have soon turned to disappointment as the Manchester was singularly unsuccessful, being plagued with engine trouble throughout its short operational career. However it was in production and the Hampdens were getting old, so re-equipment of squadrons and formation of new ones went on. 97 Sdn, at Waddington in World War I, reformed there on Manchesters in February, moving next month to Coningsby, but 44, 49, 61, 83, 106 and 144 soldiered on with Hampdens throughout 1941.

22 *Handley-Page Hampden, 5 Group standard equipment in the early war years. This example is a 50 Sdn aircraft, at Swinderby.* (50 Sdn).

In December 1941 a significant event took place at Waddington. The Manchester, having been redesigned to take four Rolls-Royce Merlin engines, re-emerged as the Lancaster, an aircraft which was to become forever associated with Lincolnshire. 44 Sdn at Waddington was selected as the first unit, having just been officially titled 44 (Rhodesia) Sdn, a quarter of its strength coming from that country. The first Lancaster operation was on 3 March, laying mines in the Heligoland Bight, while on 28 April a low level raid against the MAN diesel works at Augsburg gained Sdn Ldr Nettleton the VC. 44 became the envy of 5 Group, and Coningsby became the next Lanc station, 97 and 106 converting during January and May respectively. Their stay was brief though, 97 moving to the new airfield at Woodhall Spa in March and 106 to Syerston in September. Coningsby then closed in order to have concrete runways built. The early war built stations, from late 1940 on, were temporary affairs, accommodation being hutted and, together with bomb dumps, hangars and workshops, distributed around the perimeter of the airfield and in the surrounding countryside. Runways were not provided until the arrival of the Lancaster, Halifax and Stirling made them essential if operations were to be carried out during the winter months.

At the other 5 Group stations, changes were also taking place. Hemswell was transferred to 1 Group, whose HQ was now at Bawtry near Doncaster, and the two Hampden squadrons, 61 and 144, left in July 1941, being replaced by the Polish squadrons, 300 and 301 from Swinderby. At Waddington 207 Sdn left in November and was replaced by a Canadian bomber unit 420 (RCAF) Sdn, still with Hampdens. 1942 at Scampton saw 49 Sdn, one imagines reluctantly, receive Manchesters in April (though Lancs arrived in June), while 83 Sdn left in August to be replaced by the Lancs of 57 Sdn. F/Lt Learoyd of 49, and Sgt Hannah of 83, were both awarded the VC while stationed at Scampton. 467 (RAAF) Sdn formed with Lancs in November, leaving the same month for Bottesford.

5 Group opened two new stations during 1942, Woodhall Spa and Skellingthorpe which received 50 Sdn with Lancs. Skellingthorpe had had a period as a satellite of Swinderby and Swinderby itself had transferred to 5 Group. The Polish squadrons had bombed Berlin for the first time in February 1941 and had gained fame from their frequent mentions by the media, 'Polish' being immediately identifiable. 1 Group's move from Hucknall, Notts to Bawtry meant a reallocation of the Lincolnshire stations and the Poles left for Hemswell when Swinderby came under 5 Group in July 1941. They were replaced by 50 Sdn and 455 (RAAF) Sdn, both with the elderly Hampden. 455 was the first Australian bomber squadron to form in Britain. 50 Sdn actually moved on 18 July, and flew its first Swinderby operation on the night of 20/21st, such was the intensity of bombing at this time. 455, after several vicissitudes, became operational in September and the two squadrons continued to raid Europe. As at many other airfields, accommodation was strained and the weather had held up building. In November 50 Sdn moved to Skellingthorpe while the runways were built at Swinderby. 455 left to convert to torpedo dropping in April and 50 Sdn moved back to Swinderby in June 1942, now with Manchesters, F/O Manser having received the posthumous award of the VC while the squadron was at Skellingthorpe. Two humourous stories are told of the 455 Sdn personnel at Swinderby. One disconsolate Aussie, surveying the steadily falling rain, exclaimed "Jeez, if they cut the barrage balloon cables, the bloody place would sink"; while a compatriot, before Newark Magistrates for poaching, told the JP that "My grandfather was deported to Australia for poaching and I'm hoping you'll give me the same sentence". Skellingthorpe, having proved unsatisfactory during 50 Sdn's detachment, was now brought up to scratch and 50 Sdn moved back there in October. At the end of 1942, the 5 Group line up in Lincolnshire was, Waddington - 44 Sdn and 9 Sdn both with Lancasters; Skellingthorpe - 50 Sdn, Lancasters; Scampton - 49 and 57 Sdns, Lancasters; Woodhall Spa - 97 Sdn, Lancasters.

23 *One of the 50 Sdn Avro Manchesters at Swinderby or Skellingthorpe in the summer of 1942.* (50 Sdn).

As already mentioned, 1 Group had taken over the northern Lincolnshire bomber stations, Hemswell and Binbrook. At Hemswell the Poles still had Wellingtons, as did 12 and 142 Sdns at Binbrook. July 1941 saw another old World War I airfield re-open, Elsham Wolds, which received 103 Sdn Wellingtons from Newton, Notts. 103 was to stay at Elsham for the rest of the war, re-equipping briefly with Halifaxes in 1942 before it was decided that the Lanc should be 1 Group's aircraft, and 103 received these. The next new station was Grimsby, built on the site of the pre-war flying club airfield, and which re-opened in November 1941 for the Wellingtons of 142 Sdn from Binbrook, leaving just 12 Sdn at that air-field. 1942 saw the additions of Ingham in May, Wickenby in September, and Kirmington in October. Like 5 Group this meant a shuffle among the squadrons, and 1 Group order of battle in December 1942 was Wickenby, 12 Sdn, Lancasters; Grimsby, 100 Sdn, Lancasters; Elsham Wolds, 103 Sdn, Lancasters; Kirmington, 142 and 150 Sdns, still with Wellingtons; Ingham, 300 Sdn, Wellingtons; Hemswell, 301 and 305 Sdns, Wellingtons and Blyton, 199 Sdn, Wellingtons. A strange footnote to Lincolnshire's early bomber operations is that, in May 1943 the latest type of Junkers Ju88 night fighter landed at Dyce airfield, Aberdeen, flown by a German night fighter pilot Heinrich Schmitt who was, sur-prisingly, a British agent. The full story of this is told in *The Great Coup* by Robert Hill, published 1978 by Arlington Books. After the war

Schmitt was interviewed by a German newspaper and in this interview claimed he had landed a Dornier Do217 at 'RAF Lincoln' (Waddington), on the night of 20 May 1941, to deliver a package to a waiting RAF officer. He claimed that this landing was official, on behalf of the Luftwaffe, and that other German pilots also landed in Britain, by arrangement, carrying peace proposals.

Coastal Command

North Coates had been evacuated by 1 Air Observers School on the outbreak of war, and for the first few months of the war housed only ground units, presumably because of fear of invasion or possibly because of Coastal Command's lack of squadrons. The ground units included 2 Recruit Training Pool and 1 Ground Defence School, which trained airmen in the art of airfield defence; but flying returned in February with the arrival of two of Coastal Command's long range fighter squadrons, 235 and 236, both with fighter versions of the Blenheim. These two units patrolled far out over the North Sea and were joined by a similar unit, 248 Sdn, in March. By May all had left to help out Fighter Command in the south. The station now assumed the role it was to carry out for the rest of the war, attacking enemy shipping, and it fell to 22 Sdn to open the proceedings. 22 Sdn was re-formed in the torpedo-bomber role in 1934 and had been the first squadron to replace its elderly Vildebeest biplanes with the brand new Bristol Beaufort. In April 1940 the Beauforts touched down at North Coates and the crews continued to train on them.

The other new unit, arriving in May, was 812 Sdn Fleet Air Arm, whose Fairey Swordfish appeared very antiquated compared with 22 Sdn aircraft, but both units operated across the North Sea bombing German ports and shipping. In April 1941 22 Sdn sent a detachment to St Eval, Cornwall, and from there attacked the German battlecruiser 'Gneisenau' in Brest Harbour. In this operation F/O Keith Campbell was awarded a posthumous VC. 22 Sdn was replaced by its sister unit 42 Sdn, also with Beauforts, while 812 was relieved by another Fleet Air Arm Swordfish Sdn, 816. Both were replaced in June by 86 Sdn, another Beaufort anti-shipping squadron, 812 and 816 Sdns were the only operational FAA units based in Lincolnshire during the war. Yet another Canadian unit, 407 Sdn, now arrived in Lincolnshire, equipped with the Lockheed Hudson, an anti-submarine and shipping strike aircraft. Anti-shipping strikes were dangerous operations, conducted at sea level with no room for error, and 407 became expert, damaging 150,000 tons of enemy shipping in its three months at North Coates. The new AOC Coastal

Command, Sir Philip Joubert, had put a stop to the bombing raids on German ports, leaving these attacks to Bomber Command, while Coastal concentrated on shipping.

October saw two non-operational units arrive to share the airfield, which by now had got rather congested, necessitating the opening of a relief airfield at Donna Nook. Donna never had units officially based on it but took North Coates overspill. 6 Anti-Aircraft Co-operation Unit (AACU) was equipped with Lysanders and, as its title suggests, towed targets with which to give practice to the Army's A/A gunners, while 278 Sdn operated Lysanders, Ansons and Walrus amphibians on air-sea rescue duties along the Lincolnshire and Yorkshire coasts, working closely with 22 Motor Launch Unit at Grimsby. 22 MLU was the RAFs only air-sea rescue launch unit based in the county, the next down the coast being at Wells-next-the-Sea in Norfolk. Helping to fill this large gap was, of course, Skegness lifeboat. Both aircraft and launch ASR units did extremely important work, not least in helping the morale of aircrew operating over the cold North Sea, who knew they now had a fighting chance of rescue if forced to ditch.

86 and 407 left North Coates in February 1942 and were replaced by two Hudson squadrons, 53 and 59, and another Beaufort unit, 217, while the FAA sent a second line unit, 776 Sdn, equipped with the unusual Blackburn Roc. 6 AACU was replaced by a 7 AACU detachment. The Hudson squadrons exchanged in May for 206 and 224 Sdns, and also in May came 415 (RCAF) Sdn. Their aircraft was one very familiar to Lincolnshire folk, the Hampden, but with an unfamilar role, as torpedo bomber. By mid 1942 the anti-shipping strike units had proved their worth against the enemy's shipping which skirted the north German and Low Country coasts. A new concept was now to be tried, the Strike Wing. North Coates was selected to house the first of these, three Beaufighter squadrons assembling at the station during the autumn. Each was assigned a particular task, and the Wing was intended to operate as an entity; 143 Sdn had the normal cannon and machine-gun armed Beaus and was to concentrate on suppressing enemy return fire from the escort ships; 236 Sdn had Beaufighters doing the same with bombs, while 254 had torpedo-armed Beaus for attacking the merchant ships. On 20 November, 236 and 254 Sdns mounted the Wings first op, against a convoy of 12-16 ships heading for Rotterdam. A combination of circumstances led to the loss of three Beaus with four more seriously damaged, for only three hits on the ships, an inauspicious start. The C-in-C immediately withdrew the Wing from operations for further training.

Training

Most of Lincolnshire's training units were withdrawn westwards on the outbreak of war, but four Training Command Stations remained in the county. Before detailing their activities it is necessary to outline the RAF flying training system as it stood in 1942. Pilots started their flying training at Elementary Flying Training Schools where they learnt the basics of flying, generally on Tiger Moths or Magisters; on satisfactory completion of this stage they moved on to advanced flying training — these schools were known as Service Flying Training Schools until 1942, then (Pilot) Advanced Flying Units. Depending on the ability and predilection shown by the pilots at EFTS, they went to single engined (P)AFUs (Harvards or Masters) or twin engined (P)AFUs (usually Oxfords). Often these stages were carried out overseas under the Empire Air Training Scheme, and many schools in fact moved overseas. However, it was found that flying in British weather and the congested British airspace meant that pilots trained overseas needed to familiarize themselves with these conditions, and so some (P)AFUs served this purpose. After AFU the pilot moved on to an Operational Training Unit, where he flew, as far as was possible, the aircraft he was destined to fly on operations, and learnt air fighting tactics, gunnery etc. At OTU the bomber pilot teamed up with his navigator, who had come through Air Observer School (later (Observer) Advanced Flying Unit), wireless operator (from Radio School), bomb aimer (AOS and Bombing and Gunnery School), and gunners (Air Gunnery School). All of these airmen were put together in a hangar and left to sort themselves into crews. From OTU, until 1942, the crews went straight to their squadrons, but with the advent of the four engined heavy bombers, a further stage was introduced, the Heavy Conversion Unit, and here the crew were joined by the flight engineer and a further gunner making the seven needed for the Lancaster or Halifax. Because Lancasters were in short supply, the HCUs operated Stirlings and Halifaxes. Day fighter pilots went from a Spitfire or Hurricane OTU straight to a squadron, but night fighter pilots teamed up with a radar observer at night fighter OTU. There was a similar pattern for Coastal Command crews and, later in the war, for transport crews. Pilots selected to be flying instructors went to Flying Instructors School (FIS).

Lincolnshire's part in this programme took several forms. Cranwell had always been a large camp, and World War II saw it filled to overflowing. The RAF College, on 3 September 1939, was renamed the RAF College Flying Training School, and carried out the same work as the other SFTSs, equipped with Oxfords. By the spring of 1941, again in common with the other SFTSs, RAF CFTS was flying a fantastic number of aircraft by today's standards (150 Oxfords) necessitating relief airfields at

Fulbeck and Barkston. Nor was the FTS the only occupant — 1 E & W School became 1 Signals School, then 1 Radio School, training both air and ground wireless operators and equipped with Wallaces, Valentias, DH 86Bs and Mentors, before standardizing on Proctors and Dominies. In September 1940 2 FIS formed with Tutors and Oxfords, becoming 2 Central Flying School in November and leaving in the summer of 1941. The Hospital, at Cranwell since 1922, was moved from this noisy and crowded environment to Rauceby mental hospital, which grew to house 1,000 beds at its peak, plus a Burns Unit where Sir Archibald MacIndoe often operated. A rather unusual addition to Cranwell's occupants was 3 (Coastal) OTU which arrived in August 1941 equipped mainly with Whitleys, a type new to the county. 3 OTU trained Coastal Command crews in operational techniques, and converted them to the Whitley. Bombing and gunnery training was carried out and a feature of the course were the long cross-country flights, including a set one to Rockall which involved 980 miles of flying. Some overseas flights were also made. It was a 3 OTU Whitley which caused the most serious war damage to the College building when in March 1942 it hit the roof in fog, killing three crew, and one student in the college. Otherwise, although aircraft were attacked in the circuit by intruders, Cranwell escaped lightly. A change of role resulted in half of the FTS Oxfords being replaced by Masters in January 1942, the school now, unusually, running both single and twin-engined courses. Ground units at Cranwell during this period were HQ 21 Gp Training Command, School of Clerks Accounting (to 1941), Equipment Training School (to June 1941) and a Supplies Depot.

Despite the undoubted value of Cranwell's training role, in retrospect the station's most important contribution to the history of the RAF and its future took place in May 1941. On 11 May, a small, partially dismantled aircraft arrived by road, followed later by a team of engineers led by one of Cranwell's 'Old Boys', W/C Frank Whittle:

'I had not flown since June 1939, so I took the opportunity to borrow an Avro Tutor from 2 CFS. I was very pleased to feel that I felt completely at home . . . . On the morning of the next day, the 15th May, the weather was quite unfit for test flying, and so I returned to Lutterworth. But when I returned the weather was improving, I hurried back to Cranwell in the evening, by which time the weather had improved to the point where it was suitable for the flight. It was by no means ideal, but there was some blue sky and the cloud base had lifted considerably. While the E28 taxied to the extreme eastern end of the runway, a group of us went by car to a point about 400 yards along the runway. Sayer [Gerry Sayer, test pilot] was in position at about 7.40 p.m. He ran the engine up to 16,500 r.p.m. against the brakes. He then released the brakes and the aircraft quickly gathered speed and lifted smoothly from the runway after a run of about 600 yards. It continued to the west in a flat climb for several miles, and disappeared from view behind cloud banks'.

(Whittle F *Jet* Muller, 1953)

53

This was the first flight by a British jet aircraft, the Gloster/Whittle E28, and was completely successful. Cranwell was chosen because of its comparative closeness to Whittle's Powerjet factory at Lutterworth, Leics, and for its long runway and clear approaches. It was also a particularly appropriate choice, as it was there, as a Cadet, that Frank Whittle wrote the thesis which first turned his thoughts to the jet engine. Various trial flights were made under stringent security arrangements, but the RAF personnel, of course, noticed this strange aircraft. Whittle records

> *'One officer at least was greatly disturbed by what he had seen. He sat in the Officers' Mess with a puzzled frown. When asked what was troubling him, he replied that he had seen a strange aeroplane "Going like a bat out of hell" and there was something odd about it, but he couldn't think what it was. After a pause, he said "My God! chaps, I must be going round the bend — it hadn't got a propellor!"'*

The E28 was later fitted with a developed engine, and its flights were then carried out from a new airfield at Edgehill, Warwickshire.

Sutton Bridge had been evacuated by 3 ATS on the outbreak of war and briefly gained an operational role with the arrival of 64 Sdn Blenheim fighters during August 1939. It also saw the formation in October of two fighter squadrons, 264 and 266. 264 was destined to be the first Defiant unit, but teething troubles delayed delivery of the aircraft until after the squadron had moved to Martlesham Heath in December. It was to suffer heavy losses in the Battle of Britain. 266 did not receive any aircraft until December and then only makeshift fighters, Fairey Battles. Spitfires arrived in January 1940 and the squadron worked up before leaving, also for Martlesham, in March 1940, seeing action over Dunkirk and in the Battle of Britain. Having housed operational Spitfires, Sutton Bridge now received training Hurricanes, as 6 OTU formed in March. The OTU trained newly qualified pilots to fly and fight the Hurricane and in November, in common with the other fighter OTUs, had 50 added to its number, becoming 56 OTU. This OTU played an important part in helping to replace the heavy fighter pilot losses in the first years of the war, but moved to Scotland in March 1942. The replacement unit was the Central Gunnery School which operated a variety of aircraft on which to train air gunnery instructors and to run specialised gunnery courses. Jack Bushby was sent on a course from 83 Sdn at Waddington.

> *'Royal Air Force, Sutton Bridge, at first sight gave the impression that, in its remote corner of the fen country, no-one had yet broken the news to it that the war had started nearly three years before. A smallish grass airfield, it lay to one side of the ruler-straight River Nene running right through the fens and carrying the drainage water out to be lost among the sandbanks of the Wash.*

A small, untidy village straggled on the other bank, and the two were con-nected by a bridge. On a convenient open space, in the middle of the village, temporary accommodation huts had been erected and it was but a few minutes walk from these across the bridge to the airfield offices and hangars. These latter housed the antique Wellington and Hampden which formed the aircraft of the Central Gunnery School; whilst in another hangar stood about half a dozen Spitfires . . . . The course itself went deep into the theory of aerial gun-nery and the mechanics of guns, turrets and the mysteries of ballistics. There was plenty of flying in the Hampden and the Wellington, putting theory into practice, not only at live targets but also conducting fierce mock battles against attacking Spitfires from the Fighter end of the school, using camera guns . . . . However, the principle exercises laid on for our delight were those known as Full Scale Tactical Formation Defence. Now these were grand occasions when the entire school strength of three Hampdens and three Well-ingtons would become airborne in an imposing circus which flew majestically over the flat fen country at some point along its route to be attacked by the Spitfires'.

Grantham started the war equipped with Ansons, Harts and Audaxes, and was brought up to a personnel strength of 927 in September 1939. By November the FTS was operating 105 aircraft, flying 2,800 day hours and 100 at night during that month. This number of aircraft was the norm for an FTS, and to this total could be added the Tutor, Oxford and Magister of 5 Group Communications Flight, used to ferry the 'St Vincents' officers around 5 Group airfields. By July 1940 Fairey Battles had replaced the biplanes, and 12 SFTS operated 64 Ansons and 48 Bat-tles, Harlaxton having re-opened as a relief landing ground. 5 Group Comm Flight also received new equipment, Percival Proctors. In the autumn of 1940 the School was warned to prepare for a move to Canada, but this was cancelled in October and training in earnest was renewed. April 1941 saw one of the School's aircraft shot down over Harlaxton by an enemy intruder; it also saw the arrival of the first Oxfords, which replaced the Ansons by October. The FTS now had the role of training pilots intended for night fighter training at 51 OTU, Cranfield, Beds. The OTU flew Blenheims, and so Blenheims formed the Advanced Training Squadron of 12 SFTS, the pupils doing their initial flying on Oxfords. High spirits among the pupils sometimes led to them breaking the rules, and in October 1942 a Sgt Allen was reduced to the ranks and given 21 days detention for low flying. Personnel at Grantham and Harlaxton now totalled 2,593. A similar training establishment, 15(P)AFU, lodged briefly at Kirmington during 1942.

Manby continued to house 1 Air Armament School, and early develop-ment of the new Hispano 20 mm cannon took place, a weapon fitted to all RAF fighters later in the war and lasting until the 1970s. Flying and testing were sometimes interrupted by the Luftwaffe, and the airfield's defences shot down a Junkers Ju88 in December 1940. In mid 1940 2 Ground Armament School formed to train the armourers and bomb disposal squads, but this unit left for Lancashire in November 1941. The original Battles were beginning to be replaced by Blenheims and Wellingtons, and the increase in activity saw Manby using Caistor as a satellite from December 1942. Caistor had been used by Kirton-in-Lindsey's fighters until then. Jack Bushby arrived at Manby for A/G training in 1941 and found it had

'efficient administration and a strict discipline, to give it the time honoured soubriquet, bags of bull. It was the home of air armament and contained not only a Gunnery School but also ran specialist courses for Armament Officers and sundry other explosive activities. There were three thousand officers and airmen and everyone thought, lived and breathed armament . . . . We were marched down to the Stores there to be issued with a small triangular piece of white linen to slip into the front of our side caps, thus to signify aircrew under training. 'Aircrew under training' indeed! Just wait until the girls in Louth got a load of this. In truth the young ladies of that sleepy market town had seen so many sprog airmen come and go over the last year or two that they were now completely immune and blasé to any glamorous connotation . . . . We sat in ground rig training turrets and twirled, rotated, elevated and depressed until we were dizzy . . . . We spent hours on a cold windswept part of the coastal sand dunes firing at cardboard Me 109's a half mile away . . . . In its instruction, as in its discipline, Manby was thorough. There were other gunnery schools but Manby was the original and the best and it was soon made plain to 32 Course how lucky it was to be there'.

(Bushby J *Gunner's Moon* Ian Allan, 1972)

Part Four

World War II — the later years 1943-1945

Bomber Operations

After 3½ years of war Bomber Command was developing into a mighty force and its new aircraft, weapons and navigation aids were all contributing to greater effectiveness. The first 1,000 bomber raid had been carried out against Cologne in May 1942; Lancasters and Halifaxes were coming from the factories in large numbers, fitted with the new Gee and H2S target finding equipment; 8 (Pathfinder Force) Group had been formed, immediately increasing bombing accuracy; and, last but not least, Arthur Harris was now C-in-C. Bomber Command's role was also made clear by the Casablanca Conference Directive of January 1943. Together with the US 8th Air Force, it was to be used

> *'for the progressive destruction and dislocation of the German military, industrial and economic system, and the undermining of the morale of the German people to the point where their capacity for armed resistance is fatally weakened'.*

The Command gathered its resources for this task. In March 1943 Lincolnshire's bomber stations were:

No. 1 Group:

Wickenby, 12 Sdn, Lancaster; Grimsby, 100 Sdn, Lancaster; Elsham Wolds, 103 Sdn, Lancaster; Kirmington, 166 Sdn, Wellington; Ingham, 199 Sdn, Wellington; Hemswell, 300, 301 and 305 Sdns, Wellington. These bases housed a total of 57 Lancasters and 80 Wellingtons.

5 Group:

Waddington, 9 and 44 Sdns, Lancaster; Fiskerton, 49 Sdn, Lancaster; Skellingthorpe, 50 Sdn, Lancaster; Scampton, 57 Sdn, Lancaster; Woodhall Spa, 97 Sdn, Lancaster. Total: 105 Lancasters.

(The faithful Hampdens had made their last bomber operation in September 1942.)

In March 1943 Guy Gibson returned to Lincolnshire to command a new top secret unit, known as X Sdn, at Scampton. A few days later the Air Ministry allocated it a number, 617. The story of the Dams Raid in May 1943 is too well known to retell here, but it caught the public imagination, and the Squadron became known as 'The Dambusters', which name still sticks. Originally intended to be used only for the Dams raid, 617 carried on after it, although Gibson had left for a well deserved rest, the exploit having earned him Scampton's third VC. Morale was not good, as no further ops were undertaken until July when the squadron raided Italy, carrying on to North Africa, with another raid on the way back. August saw 617 move to Coningsby with its brand new runways, while sister unit 57 Sdn moved to the new airfield at East Kirkby, thus permitting Scampton to close so that it too could have concrete runways built. However, although the station did not house any squadrons, it was still HQ 52 Base and controlled the satellites of Dunholme Lodge and Fiskerton. The Base system was a new organisation introduced to simplify the chain of command and increase operational efficiency. The first digit of the Base number denoted the Group it belonged to and the second the individual airfield. Each Base consisted of an HQ and one or two satellites, the HQ controlling operations and housing the Base Major Servicing Unit. During its non-flying days Scampton housed the Aircrew Commando School, which moved in from Morton Hall near Swinderby (leaving the Hall to become HQ 5 Group, which moved in from 'St Vincents', Grantham). The School served to physically toughen newly arrived aircrew, and train them in survival and evasion should they be shot down over Europe.

New bomber airfields were opening almost monthly during 1943. On 14 April Bardney received the Lancasters of 9 Sdn, which took off from Waddington the previous evening bound for Spezia, Italy. The ground crew left Waddington at 9 pm and the aircraft landed back at Bardney at 6.30 am; such was the pace of the bomber offensive. Dunholme Lodge opened in May, and 44 (Rhodesia) Sdn arrived from Waddington which then, like Scampton, got its concrete runways. 44 used up the stock of the Aircrew Sergeants Mess at an enormous party the night before the move! Over on the Wolds, June saw 101 Sdn fly into Ludford Magna, its home for the remainder of the war. Ludford soon rejoiced in the nickname 'Mudford Magna' as, like all the other war construction airfields, mud was ever present after wet weather. Its near neighbour Kelstern, opened in October and its squadron, like 617, was a completely new unit without the traditions and service of squadrons like 44, 100 and 101. This made no difference at all to its morale, and 625, with its motto 'We avenge', operated Lancasters throughout its commission and, after

24 *HQ, 5 Group, Bomber Command, 1937-43. 'St Vincents', Grantham, a recent picture showing the house with the operations block to the right.* (Ogden, Dodd & Welch).

the war, was one of the first squadrons to erect a memorial to its fallen members on the site of Kelstern. At the southern end of the Wolds, Spilsby had opened in September, housing 207 Sdn while Metheringham (106 Sdn), and North Killingholme (550 Sdn) joined the order of battle before the year's end.

Despite the fact that all the RAF bomber squadrons were extremely cosmopolitan, being composed of British, Commonwealth and Allied aircrews, the Commonwealth countries did form their own squadrons, numbered in the 400 series. Some of the Canadian units, both fighter and bomber, had already served in the county, but the Canadian bomber squadrons had all moved to Yorkshire bases to form 6 (Canadian) Group, Bomber Command. The Australians had not the requisite number of units to do this, many Aussie airmen remaining at home to fight the Japanese. However, they did form 3 Lancaster squadrons all of which were operating in Lincolnshire by 1944; (there was also one Halifax squadron in 4 Group).

460 Sdn had served for a year at Breighton, Yorkshire.

'After having been at Breighton for over a year the squadron had really become a part of that normally peaceful section in the East Riding of Yorkshire . . . . The people of Breighton looked upon them as their protegé, and were grieved at their losses and tolerant of their pranks . . . . On 14 May the transfer to Binbrook officially took place. The aircrews and maintenance personnel flew over in Lancasters, whilst the main body were transported by Horsa gliders. [This was a quick method of moving, and provided much needed practice for the Army glider pilots and their tow tugs]. Binbrook, their new home, was situated on the top of the highest point of the Lincolnshire countryside, and it proved bitterly cold in winter, for, apart from the snow, it caught the full blast of the winds whipping in from the North Sea. However, despite the comparatively harsh climatic conditions, Binbrook being a peacetime station provided many comforts which were certainly not available at Breighton. The crews were billeted in what were peacetime married quarters, and both the officers and sergeants mess had the reputation of providing the best meals available at any RAF station in England.

The squadron settled comfortably into the life at Binbrook, the favourite pub being the "Marquis of Granby" . . . . "Smokey Joe's", an old hut about halfway between the station and village, had been converted into a restaurant of sorts, and used to dish out tea and baked beans on toast during the idle moments of day or night'.

460 was soon back on ops, the first being two days after the move and the second taking part in a raid on Dortmund when Bomber Command dropped, for the first time, over 2,000 tons of bombs. Two Australian

crews were lost from the 22 taking part. The squadron was to lose 48 more crews during the rest of 1943, from 67 operations, each crew composed of seven airmen.

Not all the action took place in the air however — bomb explosions on the airfields were fortunately rare, but did take place, causing much damage, and shaking the local communities. At Binbrook in July 1943, an electrical short circuit caused the entire bomb load of one Lancaster to fall to the ground, causing the incendiaries to burn.

'Two of the ground staff were inside the bomber at the time and they leapt out and tried to roll the 4,000lb (Cookie) bomb away, but found it was hopeless and ran for safety. They had gone about 400 yards when the Cookie together with two 1,000lb bombs exploded, scattering the incendiaries among the other aircraft and knocking the two escaping airmen to the ground. The Lancaster standing in the next dispersal point burst into flames and about two minutes later its bomb load exploded'.

Due to brave work by ground staff, further explosions were averted, and in half an hour the danger was past; 17 Lancasters later took off for Cologne. Last word must rest with Group Captain Hughie Edwards, VC, Binbrook's CO, who

' . . . . swore that whilst going from one bomber to another in his staff car, he was doing about 50 and was passed by an RAF erk running from the danger area!!'.

Accidents on take off also happened to the bombers and, fully laden with fuel and bombs as they were, usually proved fatal. Flt Lt Knyvett of 460 took off on the first op of his second tour (all crews had to do a tour of 30 operations), on 2 January 1944. Knyvett —

'crashed immediately after take off, apparently as a result of some technical defect, because he was never in control of the aircraft during the short time it was airborne. He pleaded over the radio telephone with Gp Captain Edwards, watching from the control tower, to advise him what to do, but before he had a chance to reply the lurching bomber, fully laden with bombs and petrol, crashed after doing half a circuit and killed the whole crew. A WAAF, also standing in the control tower, was carried away hysterical after hearing the screams of the doomed crew over the R/T just as they crashed'.

Such was the price bomber crews paid, and because of these dangers, they played hard and drank hard. Every squadron had its favourite local pub, such as the 'Marquis of Granby', Binbrook; 'White Hart', Lissington; 'The George', Langworth; 'Horse & Jockey', Waddington; 'Abbey Lodge', Kirkstead; 'Petwood Hotel' and 'Golf Hotel', Woodhall Spa; the 'Ship' and the 'Callow Park', Skegness; 'Shades', Spilsby;

'Peacock & Royal', Boston; 'Houghton Arms', Timberland, and many others. In Lincoln the 'Saracens Head' and 'Ye Olde Crowne' were the haunts of all the Lincolnshire squadrons. Parties were held at the slightest excuse and 460 held one —

> 'in the dance hall on the pier at Cleethorpes . . . . Almost 1,000 people attended, and it was paid for by the aircrews as a gesture to the ground staff . . . . As the evening wore on and became more rowdy, one intrepid type decided to dive off the end of the pier but overlooked the fact that the tide was at low ebb, with the result that he landed with a sickening thud on his head in the sand. His pulse rate is reported to have dropped to an alarming 34 for some time, but he lived, and a relieved M.O. said he didn't think this could happen to any other squadron'.
>
> (Firkins P *Strike and Return* Paterson Brokensha Pty Ltd, Perth Australia)

1943 passed into 1944, the offensive continued, and the Lincolnshire squadrons were out each night the weather permitted. Most of the squadrons flew the normal raid, loaded with HE bombs and incendiaries, but there was the odd squadron which had 'special duties' — not those usually connected with this term, which entailed dropping agents and supplies to occupied Europe — but those different from the normal main force raids. 617 was of course one of these. Arthur Harris had decided 'We'll make 'em a special duties squadron. They needn't do ordinary ops, but whenever the Army or Navy want a dam or a ship or something clouted we'll put 617 on to it'. Sir Ralph Cochrane, AOC 5 Group, carried this a stage further and got 617 training with the new Stabilising Automatic Bomb Sight, from altitudes of 20,000 ft. The bomb load was to be the 10 tonner, designed by Sir Barnes Wallis, which only the Lancaster could carry. The Dambusters trained over Wainfleet range and were now under the command of Leonard Cheshire. In January 1944 they moved from Coningsby to the tree-surrounded Woodhall Spa and all the time were evolving new techniques, culminating in low level marking by Cheshire himself; this was used very successfully when 12 Lancs from the squadron flattened the Gnome-Rhône aircraft engine factory at Limoges (using the normal types of bombs), without damaging the surrounding French housing.

In April two Mosquitoes were loaned to 617 for target marking, being much more manoeuvrable than the heavy Lancaster. Later still, Cheshire was to use a Mustang. An unusual job for the squadron was to fly, extremely accurately, slowly advancing orbits across the Channel on the evening of D-Day minus One, throwing out 'window' to simulate, on enemy radar, an invasion force moving at 12 knots towards Calais, a spoof which was completely successful. Shortly afterwards it took a more active part in the invasion by dropping the first Tallboy bombs on the Saumur railway tunnel, cutting a vital reinforcement link to the Germans in Normandy. In September the first raid was made on the 'Tirpitz', anchored in a Norwegian fjord; the squadron operated from a Russian base for this. Second and third attacks were needed before the German battleship capsized after being hit, and surrounded, by the 12,000lb Tallboys. March 1945 saw the first use of Barnes Wallis' even larger bomb, the 22,000lb Grand Slam when 617 dropped it on the Bielefeld Viaduct. The bombsight used by 617 was extremely accurate; after the war F/O Muhl's crew dropped a Tallboy on the U-boat pens at Bremen, to test its penetrating power. A black 20ft square was painted on the top of the pens and the bomb (not fused) hit almost in the middle of it.

25 *A typical WWII Lancaster crew, from 617 Sdn, Woodhall Spa, in 1945. Left to right are F/O Harrison (navigator), Flt Sgt Garrod (engineer), F/O Muhl (bomb aimer), F/O Spiers (pilot), unknown (wireless operator), F/O Lloyd (mid-upper gunner) and Flt Lt Carroll (tail gunner). Their Lanc sports the faired-over nose turret and cut away bomb-bay of the 'Tallboy' carrying version.* (Trevor Muhl).

The other squadron which used Tallboys, and operated with 617 on all three raids against the 'Tirpitz', was 9 Sdn at Bardney, whose aircraft were named after various alcoholic beverages — eg, 'Johnny Walker' 'Youngers'. 9 Sdn was selected for the 'Tirpitz' raids because of the accuracy of its practice bombing on the ranges, and also bombed dams, bridges and viaducts. On 1 January 1945, it was ordered to mount a fourth attack on the quickly repaired Dortmund-Ems canal. Two of the ten aircraft crashed on take off and one Lanc which had just bombed was hit by flak. Flt Sgt Thompson, the W/OP, rescued the mid-upper gunner from his burning turret and then, although badly burned and frostbitten, pulled the rear gunner out of his turret, which also was on fire. The captain, F/O Benton, crashlanded in liberated Europe, but Flt Sgt Thompson died three weeks later, receiving a posthumous VC.

The third 'special' squadron was 101 at Ludford Magna, which from October 1943 undertook what is now known as electronic counter measures. All of its Lancasters carried 'Airborne Cigar' radios, (ABC), which searched out the radio frequencies used by German night fighters and then transmitted noises which effectively jammed any enemy broadcast. They also carried an eighth crew member, a German speaking radio-op, who gave the German night fighters misleading instructions in their own language. All this was carried out on top of normal bombing ops, and because the Germans could sometimes home onto the aircraft's radio transmission, 101 suffered above average losses. Some of the 'special' W/OPs were in fact German born and thus took a double risk when flying over Germany.

26 *Avro Lancaster, W-Whisky of 101 Sdn at Ludford Magna, showing the two ABC aerials.* (101 Sdn).

The night bombing offensive took a heavy toll of the crews, especially in late 1943 and the first few months of 1944, until the offensive was switched to the bombing of tactical targets prior to D-Day. 460 Sdn, for example, lost 39 crews from January to June 1944, but only 44 during the rest of the war.

Martin Middlebrook's excellent book *The Nuremberg Raid* paints an authentic picture of a typical operation, on the night of 30 March 1944, one of Bomber Command's costliest. In all, 96 aircraft failed to return out of a total despatched of 779. The effort of the Lincolnshire squadrons was thus:- 9 Sdn, Bardney, 16 sent, 1 missing; 12 Sdn, Wickenby, 14 sent, 2 missing; 44 Sdn, Dunholme Lodge, 16 sent, 2 missing; 49 Sdn, Fiskerton, 16 sent, 2 missing; 50 Sdn, Skellingthorpe, 19 sent, 3 missing, 1 crashed on take off; 57 Sdn, East Kirkby, 18 sent, 1 missing; 61 Sdn, Coningsby, 14 sent, 2 missing; 100 Sdn, Grimsby, 18 sent, all returned; 101 Sdn, Ludford, 26 sent, 7 missing; 103 Sdn, Elsham Wolds, 16 sent, 2 missing; 106 Sdn, Metheringham, 17 sent, 3 missing; 166 Sdn, Kirmington, 20 sent, 4 missing; 207 Sdn, Spilsby, 18 sent, 2 missing; 550 Sdn, North Killingholme, 17 sent, 2 missing; 576 Sdn, Elsham Wolds, 16 sent, 1 missing; 619 Sdn, Coningsby, 16 sent, 1 missing; 625 Sdn, Kelstern, 13 sent, 1 missing; 626 Sdn, Wickenby, 16 sent, all returned; 630 Sdn, East Kirkby, 16 sent, 3 missing; 460 Sdn, Binbrook, 24 sent, 3 missing; 463 Sdn, Waddington, 18 sent, all returned; 467 Sdn, Waddington, 17 sent, 2 missing. That one night, admittedly with abnormally high casualties, meant 45 empty dispersals and the staggering figure of 317 empty beds in the Lincolnshire Officers' and Sergeants' messes (248 killed, 63 prisoners and 6 who evaded capture and eventually returned home); in addition, 12 wounded airmen were in aircraft which got back to base. 101 Sdn alone lost 56 men.

What *was* a normal figure for that night was the number of aircraft despatched, the Lincolnshire squadrons sending 281 Lancasters to Nuremberg The sound of 1,124 Merlins at take off power must have made sleep impossible for many Lincolnshire residents, and this was a nightly occurrence. An evocative picture of a typical squadron take off is given by Jack Currie, just after he arrived at Wickenby to join 12 Sdn:-

'Lancaster PH-C for Charlie was lurching slowly out of dispersal, marshalled by an airman walking backwards, beckoning hands above his head. As the bomber swung on to the taxiway, the marshaller turned and ran for the grass, out of the aircraft's path. He stood, holding up his thumbs, as Charlie lumbered past, and then bent over, clasping his cap to his head, as the slipstream of the four propellors washed over him. The Lancaster moved warily along the taxiway, rudders swinging, brakes squealing, and as it passed me I

saw the mid-upper gunner's face behind his gun barrels. I put up a thumb and saw his gloved hand wave in reply. Now all around the darkening airfield the bombers were moving, making the amber taxying lamps twinkle as they passed between them, forming two processions, one from either side of the main runway, converging on the steady red light that marked the airfield controller's caravan . . . . A green light flashed from the caravan — the leading aircraft moved onto the runway, straightened into wind, paused while the engines cleared their throats, and drove, uncertainly at first and then with gathering momentum, into headlong chase for flight. As it lifted, the next Lancaster was already rolling forward, and then another, until three aircraft moved within my field of vision. The first was slowly climbing to the left, its navigation lights just visible above the tree line, the second running tail up for take off, and the third swinging on to the runway by the caravan. The air was being filled with heavy noise, which mounted to a peak as each successive bomber passed my vantage point. I put my fingers to my ears, and wondered how much noise the night could hold'.

(Currie J *Lancaster Target* New English Library, 1977)

November 1943 saw Waddington re-open, resplendent with its new runways, and at it were formed the two new Australian Lancaster squadrons, 463 and 467. 44 Sdn, from its Nissen huts at Dunholme, noted with some envy that the Aussies had moved into its former luxurious accommodation; they suggested that this was because 'if the Aussies were sent to the quagmires of Dunholme they would give more trouble than the Germans!' However, 44 was joined in the 'quagmire' by 619 Sdn in April 1944. It was now becoming more common for airfields to house two squadrons as new units joined Bomber Command. Scampton re-opened in October 1944 with 153 Sdn which had just disbanded in North Africa as a Beaufighter night fighter squadron. Still operating at night, but now with Lancs, it reformed at Kirmington and moved almost immediately to Scampton, where it stayed until disbanded at the end of the war.

Strangely, two airfields ceased to operate bombers in 1944. Ingham, which had never had runways, housed the two Polish Wellington squadrons but could not operate Lancasters, so 300 Sdn moved across to Faldingworth in March. When 300 and 305 Sdns had moved to Ingham, in June 1943, it was recorded:

'The airfield itself left much to be desired. There were no runways and the grassy area was muddy, pot-holed and bumpy all the year round — in the middle of the airfield there was a farmstead in a grove of tall but sturdy trees . . . any pilot who managed its peculiarities could be confident of landing safely in the middle of, say, Romney Marshes or Epping Forest . . . . On 1st March, 1944, some kindly soul in H.Q. Bomber Command did his good deed for the day and transferred 300 Squadron from Ingham to RAF Station, Faldingworth. Faldingworth became, by May, a fully Polish manned station, with 854 personnel, 194 of which were Polish WAAFs, and 163 aircrew'.

(Destiny Can Wait Heinemann, 1949)

Ingham then took in 1687 Bomber Defence Training Flight, whose Spits and Hurri's executed mock attacks on the bombers, giving them practice in evasion techniques. Dunholme, although having runways, was found to cause problems when Scampton re-opened, being so close that the circuits overlapped. Dunholme closed for operations in November and it was then used by General Aircraft Ltd as a modification base for their large Hamilcar gliders just coming into service, and later used in the Rhine crossing airborne operation.

For most of the Lincolnshire based squadrons the last operation of the war, rather appropriately, was against Hitler's retreat at Berchtesgaden. After this they were kept busy ferrying back POWs from Germany and taking the groundcrew to look at the damage they had helped to cause. Another mercy operation was the dropping of 6,700 tons of food to the starving Dutch civil population.

27 *The mighty Lancaster. ED 588, G-George of 50 Sdn, on a dispersal at Skellingthorpe in the summer of 1944. This aircraft flew 126 operations before being shot down in August 1944. (50 Sdn).*

In April 1945, the Lincolnshire squadron line up was as follows:

Squadron	Base	No of Lancasters
1 Group:		
12	Wickenby	23
100	Elsham Wolds	21
101	Ludford Magna	45
103	Elsham Wolds	21
150	Hemswell	21
153	Scampton	19
166	Kirmington	33
170	Hemswell	20
300	Faldingworth	21
460	Binbrook	37
550	North Killingholme	30
576	Fiskerton	31
625	Scampton	19
626	Wickenby	22
5 Group:		
9	Bardney	19
44	Spilsby	22
49	Fulbeck	20
50	Skellingthorpe	23
57	East Kirkby	15
61	Skellingthorpe	22
106	Metheringham	21
189	Bardney	22
207	Spilsby	21
227	Strubby	21
463	Waddington	19
467	Waddington	21
619	Strubby	21
630	East Kirkby	21
617	Woodhall Spa	25 + 1 Mosquito

In addition, 3 Pathfinder squadrons had been loaned to 5 Group: 83 Sdn Coningsby, 21 Lancasters; 97 Sdn Coningsby, 23 Lancasters; 627 Sdn Woodhall, 27 Mosquitos — the only non Lancaster squadron in the two Groups.

It can be seen that all the 1 and 5 Group squadrons were now Lincoln-shire based, and even before the war had finished Grimsby and Kelstern had already closed for operations, while Strubby and Fulbeck were older airfields now taken over by the bombers. Lincolnshire could, in fact, offer a grand total of 721 Lancasters and 27 Mosquitoes for operations.

When the European war ended several squadrons were earmarked for Tiger Force, the RAFs contribution to the strategic bombing of Japan, and at Swinderby 13 Aircraft Modification Unit was established to modify the Lancasters earmarked for the Force. However, two atomic bombs removed the necessity for this, and Bomber Command was now at peace. The bombers' war had lasted from the first day almost to the last, and by the end of the war they were a formidable weapon. Many criticisms have since been levelled at the strategic bombing offensive which failed to reduce Germany's production of war material as had been expected. One can only wonder at what would have happened if Bomber Command had not disrupted it. In any case, the raids forced the Germans to concentrate on fighter production, not bomber; they had to convert anti-tank guns to anti-aircraft; they had to keep the Luftwaffe largely for the defence of Germany rather than air support for the Army.

1 and 5 Groups alone, together with the nearby HCUs, lost 22,000 airmen, the names of whom are recorded in the RAF Chapel in Lincoln Cathedral. The three towers of the Cathedral, sometimes the only part showing above mist or fog, welcomed the returning crews, to whom it became a symbol. Perhaps the best tribute is paid to the bomber crews in *Royal Air Force 1939-45:*

'Those who held the controls of the bomber in their firm young hands truly deserve a crown of bays. Night after night in darkness bathed in silver or veiled with clouds, undeterred by 'the fury of the guns and the new inventions of death' they rode the skies above Germany, and paid without flinching the terrible price which war demands. In the select company of those who have laid down their lives to save the lives of others these British airmen who died bombing Germany must hold high rank. The assault, which they maintained with unswerving vigour and energy, was so well sustained, so nourished, and became so effective that the total casualties suffered by the British army in the eleven months which elapsed between its landing upon the shores of Normandy and the unconditional surrender of Germany upon the heath at Luneberg were less than the losses incurred in one month by their fathers in the battle of the Somme'.

(Richards D & Saunders H st G *Royal Air Force 1939-45* HMSO 1954*)

(*Reproduced by permission of the Controller of HMSO).

During World War II, eight VCs had been awarded to Lincolnshire based airmen: Flt Lt Roderick Learoyd, 49 Sdn, Scampton, Aug 1940; Sgt John Hannah, 83 Sdn, Scampton, Sept 1940; Sdn/Ldr John Nettleton, 44 Sdn, Waddington, April 1942; F/O Leslie Manser, 50 Sdn, Skellingthorpe, May 1942 (posthumous); W/C Guy Gibson, 617 Sdn, Scampton, May 1943; W/C Leonard Cheshire, 617 Sdn, Woodhall Spa, Sept 1944; Flt Sgt George Thompson, 9 Sdn, Bardney, Jan 1945 (posthumous); Sgt Cyril Jackson, 106 Sdn, Metheringham, April 1944.

So far in this part I have picked out the salient features of Bomber Command's war as it affected Lincolnshire, but what was life like on an average bomber airfield? Fiskerton lies half a mile across the fields from my home, five miles east of Lincoln. It was the base of two Lancaster squadrons and existed, as a flying station, from January 1943 to September 1945. Initially it was the home of 49 Sdn and was, from May 1943, a sub-station of 52 Base Scampton. There is not enough space in this book to give a full history of station or squadron, but some of the facts concerning Fiskerton are as follows.*

Operations first, as that is why the airfield existed. In August 1943, for example, 49 Sdn ops were

Aug. 2	15 A/C to Hamburg,	1 ret early, rest safe.
Aug. 9	17 A/C to Mannheim,	1 ret early, 'K' FTR.
Aug. 10	12 A/C to Nuremberg,	'B' FTR.
Aug. 12	13 A/C to Milan,	all safe.
Aug. 14	6 A/C to Milan,	1 ret early.
Aug. 15	8 A/C to Milan,	'V' FTR.
Aug. 17	12 A/C to Peenemünde,	'U' 'O' 'L' 'S' FTR.
Aug. 22	9 A/C to Leverkeusen,	all safe.
Aug. 23	9 A/C to Berlin,	all safe.
Aug. 27	12 A/C to Nuremberg,	all safe.
Aug. 30	15 A/C to München Gladbach,	all safe.
Aug. 31	16 A/C to Berlin,	1 ret early, rest safe.

Aircraft returned early because of some sort of mechanical failure in the aircraft or, occasionally, a sick crew member. On 10 September, the airfield was closed for runway resurfacing, and ops were carried out from Dunholme Lodge. Fiskerton re-opened on 24 October and operations resumed. 26 November saw aircraft 'C' crash in the circuit on return from Berlin, killing the crew. The winter months usually meant less

* See plan & key page 142

operations because of bad weather conditions. January's ops for example were:

Jan.	1	15 A/C to Berlin,	all safe.
Jan.	2	12 A/C to Berlin,	1 ret early, 'N' & 'S' FTR.
Jan.	5	6 A/C to minelaying,	all safe.
Jan.	5	5 A/C to Stettin,	all safe.
Jan.	14	9 A/C to Brunswick,	'R' FTR.
Jan.	20	12 A/C to Berlin,	all safe.
Jan.	21	10 A/C to Magdeburg,	all safe.
Jan.	21	2 A/C to spoof on Berlin,	1 ret early, other O.K.
Jan.	27	13 A/C to Berlin,	2 ret early, 'M' FTR.

A message was received from Sir Arthur Harris, C-in-C, to all groundcrew:

'On January 20, 1,030 A/C were serviceable out of I.E. strength of 1,038. When work has to be done under such trying conditions this record is almost incredible. My thanks and congratulations to all concerned in this great achievement, you are, after the crews, playing the leading part in getting on with this war'.

Those who doubt 'Bert' Harris's phrase 'such trying conditions' should contemplate intricate work on a Merlin engine 15 feet above ground, on a dispersal, in a Lincolnshire January. Hangars were luxuries reserved only for major maintenance. It is interesting to contrast these raids with those carried out in July 1944 which were against such tactical targets as 'Construction works, St Leu D'Esserent', 'railway junction, Nevers', 'enemy positions, Caen', marshalling yards, Givors', 'battle area Cohaques' and so on. Only two raids were made on Germany that month.

So the ops carried on, but Fiskerton housed 1,150 airmen and women; what of their daily life? In January 1944, 33 airmen and 3 WAAFs were 'mentioned in despatches', and in February, a station newsroom was opened in the NAAFI to enable personnel to keep up to date with the outside world. It was recorded that the RAF Central Library was providing books for serious study regarding post war careers back in civvy street. The maintenance crews, during January, checked six new aircraft delivered, and did six engine changes and 17 minor checks. Flying Control reported that the FIDO (Fog Intensive Dispersal Operation) was 'lit' on 16 January after being told that 10 USAAF Dakotas were diverting from Fulbeck due to fog; they didn't land *'due to bad navigation and disregarding of diversion instructions'.* An eleventh aircraft, en route to Fulbeck from Liverpool did land safely, though visibility off the airfield was ten yards, and a crosswind made the FIDO difficult to control; eventually, an arch of approximately 100 feet was cleared over the runway.

On the medical side, the MO reported 90 patients at Station Sick Quarters from 28 November to the end of January. He also reported that the present SSQ were *'deplorable'* and that the new quarters, under construction for six months, were urgently needed. On 11 February the whole station, except WAAFs, had an FFI inspection — all passed!

Snow and frost caused the Motor Transport section many difficulties, as vehicles froze up at dispersals, and servicing accommodation was open to the weather. The taxiway lighting also had problems due to the weather and it constantly failed due to water in the 'electrics'.

Cookhouse menus are not recorded in Fiskerton's ORB, but the Air Ministry sent a signal saying that explosives had been reported in a consignment of Spanish onions — *'all stocks are to be placed outside, at least 50 yards from any buildings'*.

Due to the distance between dispersals, offices and living accommodation, bicycles were standard RAF equipment; 11 February saw 50 new WAAFs bicycles arrive, so that *'all personnel on Technical Site now have one'*. Such transport was probably in high demand on 20 February, when Lancaster 'R' burst a tyre on take off, caught fire, and eventually blew up, fortunately without casualties. Some of the other aircraft could not take off that night and those already airborne were diverted on return to Dunholme. It is reported that wreckage from the explosion fell at Sudbrooke, two miles away, but the runway was repaired by the 25th.

March saw a Sister of Princess Mary's RAF Nursing Service talk to the WAAFs on hygiene and compliment them on *'the cleanest accommodation in 5 Group'*. The runway was blocked again on 24 March when a 101 Sdn Lancaster crashed on it. Flying Control reported

> *'Ludford A/C landed without instruction with FIDO and blocked R/W. Representation made to Ludford's Flying Control urging them to brief crews more thoroughly. Further, it has been suggested to them to illuminate the top of Stenigot wireless pylons with Sodium Flares to form a navigation aid in fog'.*

It is not recorded if this took place.

In April, Lancs which returned from an op carried one dead rear gunner, killed by a night fighter, and a bomb aimer killed by flak. The peritrack was reported to be in very bad condition, while heavy rain put a large number of the station's telephones out of action — *'the new exchange building is extremely badly built'*. Sports on the station included soccer, Canadian softball, tennis and squash, and an exchange visit with the USAAF at Langar was arranged.

21 June saw 49 Sdn, and Fiskerton's, worst night of the war, when 20 aircraft raided an oil plant at Wesseling. Six aircraft failed to return, including the CO, W/C Crocker and Flight Commander, S/Ldr Cox. The Squadron stood down for a few nights.

The taxiway was still breaking up, and 130 bays of concrete had been replaced — *'each area dug up revealed the poorness of the original work'*. This didn't stop 10 USAAF Liberators from North Pickenham in Norfolk being diverted on 22 July, and during the month 49 Sdn dropped 1,006 tons of bombs.

A major change took place on 17 October when 49 Sdn left for Fulbeck, taking most personnel with them. From 18-30 October, Fiskerton went on Care and Maintenance with a strength of 33 officers and 116 airmen, and was transferred from 5 Group control to 1 Group. 31 October saw 576 Sdn fly in from Elsham Wolds, flying its first op on 2 November to Dusseldorf, and losing two aircraft. 150 Sdn formed at Fiskerton on 1 November but transferred to Hemswell on the 22nd. 1514 Beam Approach Flight, which had been on the station since January 1944, disbanded in January 1945. In early 1945 the station personnel included 13 Australians and 3 Canadians, and the WAAFs had lectures on 'mothercraft'.

On 23 April the last bombing op took place, against SS Barracks at Berchtesgaden, 23 aircraft of 576 Sdn taking part. The squadron then flew supplies to Dutch civilians —

'for the first time in its history, the squadron was received by enthusiastic crowds throughout the target area'.

The groundcrews were flown over German cities to show them the results of their efforts on the Lancasters, and many sorties were flown to Germany and Italy to repatriate POWs and demobbed personnel. Ammunition was taken to Theddlethorpe range to be exploded, and the station began to run down. On 19 September 1945, flying by 576 Sdn ceased and the airfield was closed to flying on the 21st. During October, the Lancasters were flown away to Maintenance Units, and from 15 December the airfield went onto C & M. So ended the career of a typical Lincolnshire bomber station. Fiskerton still retains its control tower, bombing trainer, one hangar and several other buildings, although half of those frequently repaired runways and taxiways have gone. Former inhabitants still visit occasionally, as some of the writing on the wall of the control tower signifies.

Bomber support

To keep the bombers flying during World War II four things were required — aircrews, groundcrews, bombs, and petrol. Aircrew training is covered later, as is groundcrew training in the county. A fuel depot at Torksey supplied petrol for most of the Lincolnshire stations. The bombs, ammunition, and oxygen were the responsibility of three depots in the county.

93 MU opened in August 1939 on a site by Swinderby station. On the outbreak of war it was heavily camouflaged, including the roads, and began to issue bombs to Hemswell, Waddington and Scampton, having 132 airmen on staff by July 1940. When Swinderby airfield opened, the MU site was renamed Norton Disney, although this village was several miles away (the naming of RAF stations is something of a mystery — sometimes called after distant villages to confuse the enemy, as here, but then again, like Fiskerton, named after the adjacent village. On occasion the nearest village name could be confused with a station already open, and the next nearest was used). Norton Disney continued to supply 5 Group with its explosives.

100 MU, South Witham, opened in March 1942, with three officers and 90 men under canvas, five Nissen huts soon being erected. Some idea of the physical work involved at these depots can be judged by the fact that in July 1942, 3,769 tons of ammo was brought in by rail and lorry, while 1,724 tons were issued to the airfields. There was some excitement in November 1942 when a Halifax crashed and burnt 35 yards from a HE storage area! From December 1943 chemical weapons were stored, and an extra storage area for HE was established on Stretton Road. The number of airmen had risen to 211 by May 1944, when 340 railtrucks and 303 lorries delivered to the unit, and 565 lorries and 427 rail trucks were despatched. A V1 crashed and exploded nearby on 13 October 1944, and the British 'secret weapon', the Tallboy bombs, arrived for storage in February 1945.

The third depot was established as 233 MU at Market Stainton in January 1943. 267 airmen manned it, and in December 1,632 loaded rail trucks arrived plus 218 lorries, while 543 trucks and 481 lorries went out to the eastern airfields. To speed supplies to the Grimsby area a railhead was established at Brocklesby, and after much discussion with the local authorities, a chemical weapon storage site was opened at Hemingby. The first Tallboys arrived in April 1944, and the unit strength was expanded by the addition of a party of *'Italian co-operators'*, who made *'most effective tradesmen and labourers'*. Railway stations used were Donington, Hallington and Withcall, and extra sites on the disused airfields at Caistor and Goxhill were taken over in early 1945. Grand Slams were stored near the end of the war.

These MUs were dispersed over a wide area, including along the roadsides, and 233 MU had 60 miles of grass verges for storage. 233 MU closed down in 1948.

Bomber training

The training of bomber crews has already been described on page 52, and though Lincolnshire was mainly operational bombing country, Heavy Conversion Units began to form on the county's most westerly airfields. May 1942 saw the formation of the first Lancaster Conversion Unit, 1654, at Swinderby, with eight Lancs and eight Manchesters, moving to the satellite airfield, Wigsley, Notts, in June. In October the Conversion Flights of 61, 97, 106 and 207 Sdns at Swinderby formed into 1660 HCU, while January saw 1661 HCU established at Winthorpe, Notts, also Swinderby's satellite. Sgt Trevor Muhl, bomb aimer of a crew converting to Lancasters, recalls taking off from Winthorpe at 1430 hours on New Year's Eve 1942, for a two hour cross country trip. The weather was poor and once airborne the Gee navigational aid and radio both failed. Navigation suffered and the crew found themselves over the sea. Turning back for land they identified Boston and set course for base. Low cloud now obscured the ground, it was getting dark, and due to the radio failure there was no way of checking if the barometric pressure had changed. Thinking they were at 2,000 feet, the crew suddenly saw in front of them a weathercock, which they missed by application of full throttle and a frantic pull back on the stick. The trailing aerial was found later in a house at Gonerby Hill — the weathercock was attached to Grantham Church. A very shaken crew landed at 1900 hours at Wittering, to find they had been ordered to set the aircraft flying out to sea and abandon it — but, of course, this message never reached them.

Swinderby became 51 Base, HQ for the other two stations, and each of the HCUs had its own major servicing hangar at Swinderby, the Base's purpose being to co-ordinate and standardize the training of Lancaster crews for 5 Group. Initially the aircraft used were Halifaxes, Manchesters and Lancasters, but a re-organisation in 1943 which established 5 Lancaster Finishing School at Syerston, Notts, saw the HCUs re-equip with the Short Stirling. Crews trained on these and then were posted to Syerston before moving on to a squadron. In July 1944 51 Base flew its highest monthly hours, and all leave was cancelled to provide the urgently needed replacements for 5 Group. 7 (Operational Training) Group now took over Swinderby and its satellites, which became 75 Base and, in December 1944, started using Lancs to replace the Stirlings. This change meant airmen used to dodging under the turning props of the tall under-carriaged Stirling had to change their habits very quickly! 75 Base disbanded just after the war ended.

In the north of Lincolnshire, a similar organisation existed to supply 1 Group with its crews. In this case Lindholme, Yorks, was the base HQ and its two sub-stations were Blyton, 1662 HCU, and Sandtoft, 1667 HCU, both of which opened in February 1943 equipped with Halifaxes. When Sturgate opened in 1944 it acted as a relief landing ground for Blyton. As in 5 Group, the HCUs had disbanded by the end of 1945.

Fighter operations

By the beginning of 1943 the risk of a daylight attack by German raiders was negligible and consequently, the fighter squadrons at Kirton-in-Lindsey used it as a rest and training station. 303 Sdn Spits were replaced by those of 302 in February and this veteran Polish squadron was in turn replaced by one of the 'younger' Polish units, 317 Sdn. When 317 moved to Martlesham in April the station changed its role to the formal training of fighter pilots, becoming 53 OTU equipped with Spitfires. Hibaldstow, having lost its two Turbinlite squadrons, became Kirton's satellite, and it was at Hibaldstow that ACW Margaret Horton had an inadvertent flight sitting on the tail of a Spitfire, the pilot not noticing her presence until he was airborne. Fortunately both reached the ground safely after a hair raising circuit of the airfield. 53 OTU left Kirton and Hibaldstow in May 1945, when the satellite closed.

In the meantime RCAF Digby acted as a working-up and training base for the Canadian fighter squadrons although RAF squadrons also used it, including 19 and 167, both with Spitfires. Digby also kept its contact with the Belgians, begun with 609 Sdn; both the Belgian Spitfire squadrons, 349 and 350, were based at the airfield during the summer of 1943. However, it was a RCAF Station and so the Canadians were the main users; 1943 saw 411, 402 and 416 Sdns pass through, all of them returning twice during the year between ops over France. 438 Sdn was formed at Digby on Hurricanes in November, later re-equipping with the more modern Typhoon after moving to Hampshire. The pattern con-tinued during 1944 when a complete Canadian Spitfire Wing of 3 Sdns, 441, 442 and 443 formed in February, moving down to the South Coast in time to take part in the pre D-Day ops. One further nationality was added to Digby's list when, in August, 310 (Czech) Sdn came to Digby for a rest from the tactical offensive now raging. After this Digby took on a non-operational role as 116 Sdn with Oxfords, and 527 and 528 with Blenheims, performed radar calibration and other miscellaneous duties. (Lincolnshire now had three 'early warning' radar stations, Stenigot, Ingoldmells and Skendleby, and two GCI stations, Orby and Langtoft.) During the winter, ice hockey and curling were played by the Canadians and in May some former inhabitants returned from the Continent, 441 and 442 Sdns, both now equipped with Mustangs. These were Digby's last fighter squadrons and the station returned to RAF control in May. Wellingore, still a satellite of Digby, also housed mainly Canadian units, though 349 Sdn was also there. Lincolnshire's first Mustang squadron was 613, a tactical reconnaissance unit, which stayed from April to May 1943. 439 Sdn, like its sister unit 438 at Digby, formed up on Hurricanes in early 1944. Wellingore's last squadron was 402 which left in March 1944, after which the airfield ceased fighter ops.

Although the day bomber menace had almost gone by 1943, that of the night bomber was still very real, as was the threat of the German intruders operating against the returning Lancasters. When Hibaldstow closed Lincolnshire's night defence rested with Coleby Grange. 409 Sdn Beaufighters left in February 1943, being replaced by another RCAF squadron, 410, equipped with the best night fighter of all, the Mosquito.

28 *The old control tower at Coleby Grange, well preserved in 1978, and responsible during the war for Lincolnshire's night fighter defences* (Lincolnshire Library Service).

Like the day fighter squadrons, 410 was not to be solely a defensive unit, although this was its primary task. The unit was, on its move to Lincolnshire, looking forward to its first 'Ranger' operation, in which individual aircraft flew over occupied Europe shooting down aircraft, and strafing road and rail transport. In one such attack on 28 March the crew claimed one tug, two barges, six goods vans, two locomotives and two military buses! Three 'Ranger' ops were carried out per night, weather permitting, but in the defensive role a Dornier Do217 was destroyed through its own evasive action on 18 March. 27 September 1943 saw Flt Lt Cybulski and F/O Ladbrook airborne at 2012 hours for a 'Ranger' over Holland. They had turned back towards Coleby when Ladbrook got a radar contact which, on Cybulski chasing it, proved to be a Do217. Cybulski gave it a three second burst and it immediately exploded, covering the Mosquito with burning petrol and oil. Cybulski blacked out and the aircraft went into a dive. The navigator managed to regain control and the pilot, now recovered, flew back the 250 miles to base on one engine, with both feet on the rudder to counteract the good engine. When Cybulski and Ladbrook landed back at Coleby they had been airborne for 4 hours and 41 minutes, and the Mosquito was found to have all its paint burnt off, plus the fabric from the rudder. 410 left for West Malling in October and was replaced by the Mossies of 264 Sdn. They in turn were replaced by 68 Sdn, and the final night cover of the war was provided by 307 (Polish) Sdn until May 1944, when Coleby's operational role came to an end. Coleby's squadrons operated mainly under Orby GCI control, but Orby was not retained after the war and closed in August 1945.

Coastal Command

The North Coates Strike Wing trained hard after its failure in November 1942 and in the following April 143, 236 and 254 Sdns Beaufighters became operational once more, while in June the rocket-armed Beau became available; thereafter the Strike Wing usually composed up to 12 torpedo aircraft whose targets were the merchant ships, while up to 16 rocket and 8 cannon-Beaus took on the escorts. These tactics paid off and by the end of 1943 13 enemy ships totalling 34,000 tons were sunk; this success led to the formation of a second Wing at Leuchars in Scotland. North Coates Wing was reduced to two squadrons when 143 left in August 1943. Not all the sorties were carried out by as many aircraft as described above. 236 Sdn Operational Record Book records an aerial sweep on 28 January 1944, from Norderney to Schiermonnikoog — 11 aircraft of 236 Sdn took part, plus some of 254, escorted by three squadrons of Typhoons. In an unsuccessful attack on a convoy, a 236 Sdn aircraft, hit by flak, disintegrated, hitting a 254 Sdn aircraft which had to ditch. German convoys were heavily defended and the low level Beaufighter attacks sometimes proved costly; in an attack on a convoy in April aircraft 'Y' had a bullet through its starboard wing; 'S' a shell through the nose, injuring the pilot; 'P' its starboard engine cowling shot off and its port elevator and wing damaged; 'R' a hole in the starboard wing and a shell in the radio injuring the observer.

On 15 May the Wing struck at a convoy off Schiermonnikoog (an island in the Friesian chain) and in one of its most successful ops sank the one merchant vessel, an 8,000 tonner, one escort, one M class minesweeper, and left two other minesweepers on fire. 143 returned to the fold in February, but left again in May for Manston, Kent, to cover the eastern approaches to the D-Day beaches. It returned briefly in September 1944, but then left to help form a new Strike Wing at Banff in Scotland. North Coates Wing went out with a bang, as 236 and 254 sank 5 U-boats in May 1945 by which time 254 had on strength some of the Mosquito Mk XVIII, boasting a six-pounder cannon specifically designed for operations against U-boats. The Wing disbanded in May/June, its dangerous work highlighted by the fact that 484 airmen had lost their lives in ops from North Coates.

A second Coastal base opened at Strubby in April 1944 originally housing an air-sea rescue (ASR) unit 280 Sdn, the first to operate the Vickers Warwick aircraft, a successor to the Wellington bomber, performing important work in rescuing ditched airmen. The station soon took on a more offensive role, as the North Coates Wing successes had led to the formation of further Beaufighter Strike Wings. The need to restrict the enemy shipping reinforcements and supplies to France and Belgium saw the arrival of 144 and 404 Sdns to form the Strubby Strike Wing in July. They had already been in action over the Western Channel before and after D-Day. 404 was yet another of Lincolnshire's Canadian squadrons, and the two units operated in much the same way as the North Coates Wing, until the decrease in enemy shipping off the Low Countries and North Germany meant that North Coates could cope alone. 144 and 404 then departed for Dallachy, Scotland, to seek fresh targets near the Danish and Norwegian coasts and Strubby transferred to Bomber Command.

Flying training

Cranwell opened 1943 housing the RAF College FTS, operating Oxfords, Masters, Tiger Moths and Blenheims, while 3 OTU still soldiered on with the venerable Whitley. 1 Radio School had Proctors, Dominies and Oxfords. Barkston carried on as RLG until April, when it closed for runways to be laid, while Fulbeck was already being used for other purposes. Caistor and Wellingore were pressed into use as replacements. It was proving unsatisfactory to operate the large Whitleys (replaced by Wellingtons in May) alongside the many light training aircraft and in June 3 OTU moved to Pembrokeshire. The FTS trained some Turkish pilots during 1943 and in September the largest station parade ever held in the UK took place for Battle of Britain day, when 7,000 airmen and women, plus 3,000 civilians, took to the square — 10,000 in all; the mind boggles! The title RAF College Service Flying Training School, apart from its length, was also something of an anachronism and in March 1944 it was brought into line with the other FTS and retitled 17 SFTS, though its role remained the same. Spitfires, Hurricanes and Harvards joined the unit during the year but in May 1945 it transferred to Grantham.

Earlier in the war Grantham was still occupied by 12 SFTS (soon to be retitled 12 (P)AFU), with Harlaxton as its satellite, and by September 1943 was wholly equipped with Blenheims, pilots having done their initial twin-engine training on Oxfords at other (P)AFUs. An additional unit was 1536 Beam Approach Training Flight, which gave the fledgling night fighter pilots necessary training in instrument landing. Social life was quite full for the station personnel — a live ENSA show called, 'More heather breezes' was recorded as *'quite good all round, but inclined to be blue',* and also there were whist drives, a model aeroplane club at Harlaxton and concerts by Aveling-Barford's concert party. For the sporting types there was badminton, squash and snooker and the station football team beat Ruston and Hornsby 15-0. By November 1943 the grass surfaces at both Grantham and Harlaxton began to break up due to bad weather and the constant comings and goings of the Blenheims, so Balderton near Newark was used for three weeks. The situation deteriorated further and many of the Blenheims flew away to airfields in Cheshire and Lancashire. In early 1944 steel tracking was laid and the aircraft returned.

At about this time Richard Gentil arrived at 12 (P)AFU, having trained in Canada and then done an Oxford course at Shawbury, Shropshire. In his book Gentil records

'Grantham was a large station, dating from peacetime, with good amenities. The Nissen hutment area was enormous, and there was a large permanent staff'.

His course included Poles, Americans, Australians, Canadians, New Zealanders and South Africans, a microcosm of the wartime RAF. Although he was impressed by the airfield, his opinion of the town was not quite as favourable.

'It didn't take . . . long to realise that wartime Grantham was a ghastly place. It had ninety-three pubs — many of these being merely near-beer joints; just a single room with a licence to sell beer and cigarettes. All of them were packed every night either with aircrew or the nearby Army personnel. . . . The 'popsy' situation was also pretty dire, as the Servicemen far outnumbered the local females'.

The actual course involved intensive day and night flying, parachute drill (with instructors from the locally based Parachute Regiment), a spell in an oxygen tank to point out the dangers of oxygen starvation, swimming, dinghy and survival training, and so on. A trip was also arranged to the BARMC factory where the pilots saw the 20mm cannon they would eventually use being made. Accidents still happened and eight members of the course were killed, but after three months at Grantham and about 600 flying hours for each pilot, there were the celebrations before the survivors moved on to Cranfield and Beaufighters. By this time, the attractions of Nottingham had been discovered, and

'the last Nottingham-Grantham train on Sunday night was known as the 'Aircrew Express', and there has never been another train like it. It always left on time — 10.30 pm — but, as we were all boozed up to the eyeballs, negotiating the last half hour from our respective hotels always took longer than expected . . . it was the habit of the boys to leave all the train windows down to enable those who arrived at the station at just moving off time to fly . . . right past the ticket barrier on to the platform . . . so that they could hurl themselves at the window and clamber in!'

(Gentil R *Trained to intrude* Bachman & Turner, 1974)

Grantham came back into favour when Nottingham was placed out of bounds to US troops because of a VD epidemic, this fact quickly stopping British servicemen visiting the city too. In the summer of 1944 Oxfords came back on strength and there were 57 Blenheims, 30 Oxfords and 3 Ansons. February 1945 saw 12 (P)AFU move to Hixon and Cranage in the north-west Midlands.

Manby's war continued, developing new ideas and training techniques, until in July 1944 1 Air Armament School was renamed the Empire Central Armament School; this unit was

'to ensure that our armament training throughout the British Commonwealth is kept at a high progressive standard'.

To this end Manby ran the following courses — the Post-Graduate Armament Course, Advanced Armament Course, Specialist Armament Course, Bombing Leaders Course, Air Bombing Instructors Course, and the Senior NCOs Armament Instructors Course. A further change of name resulted in the Empire Air Armament School. The aircraft in use were mainly Wellingtons.

At Sutton Bridge, the Central Gunnery School continued to operate courses for Gunnery Leaders and Pilot Gunnery Instructors, but it left in February 1944 and, as the area was now considered safe from air attacks, was replaced by 7 (P)AFU, with Oxfords, which moved in from Peterborough. This unit continued to train pilots on a reduced scale to the efforts earlier in the war until April 1946 when, now titled 7 SFTS, it moved to Kirton-in-Lindsey and Sutton Bridge closed.

Non-flying units

Lincolnshire, being one of the counties nearest to the enemy and eminently suited to the building of airfields, housed very few non-flying RAF establishments, these being concentrated further west. The radar stations at Orby, Langtoft, Stenigot, Ingoldmells and Skendleby have already been mentioned, as have the ammunition MUs. There were W/T stations at Humberston and South Elkington and, at Skegness, 11 Recruits Centre. 11 RC opened in February 1941 with an establishment of 1,134. As 'HMS Royal Arthur', a Royal Navy recruit camp, was already housed at Butlins, the town must have been swamped with light and dark blue uniforms. The RAF did not have the luxury of a complete camp and various buildings were requisitioned — for example, Station Sick Quarters was in the Seacroft Boys' School, while the Abbey Hotel was one of the billets. So overcrowded did the accommodation become that 2 Wing moved to Boston. The Centre was commanded by Gp Capt Insall who had won the VC in the RFC during World War I. Even at this early stage in their RAF careers the recruits were faced with death, three being killed in a bombing raid on 15 September 1942, and another nine on the 24 October. Having sent thousands of recruits through to take part in the war 11 RC closed in October 1944.

At the beginning of the war, 1 Ground Defence School at North Coates had trained airmen in airfield defence, and these were organised into 'defence squadrons'. However, as the war progressed a better system was needed and, in December 1941, the RAF Regiment was formed, specifically responsible for the defence of airfields and other RAF stations from ground and air attacks. The RAF Regiment Depot was established at Belton Park, Grantham and remained there until August 1946. There was a Battle Training School at Anderby Creek, and Regiment Squadrons were based on most Lincolnshire airfields during the war. These airmen in fact wore khaki battledress until 1949.

A non-flying unit whose personnel were a very welcome sight to aircrew was 22 Motor Launch Unit, later 22 Marine Craft Unit, whose air-sea rescue launches were berthed in Grimsby's tidal basin. This unit rescued many airmen throughout the war and had, in January 1945, eight launches and 145 airmen on strength. A typical example of this kind of operation was carried out by HSL 2578 on 29 December 1944.

'1705 hours, proceeded to position 53.26N, 00.32E. Man in dinghy. Two Beaufighters circling. At 1800 hours approx ten miles from position, flares were seen ahead. I acknowledged with rocket. On reaching position at 1835 hours the survivor was being taken from the water by HMS Croome L62. I went alongside at 1845, taking the survivor, Flt Sgt Gregg, 236 Sdn North Coates, aboard. He was given dry clothing and his wounds treated. Flt Sgt Gregg was suffering from shock but stated he was certain navigator went down with aircraft. Moderate sea, heavy swell, fine and clear'.

By August 1945 the number of launches was down to three, and on 16 December the unit disbanded.

Another organisation that saved aircrew, and civilian lives, was the Royal Observer Corps. Although a civilian organisation, it was operationally part of Fighter Command and its members, standing watch 24 hours a day, seven days a week throughout the war, performed sterling service. The Operations Room of 11 Lincoln Group was initially (1936), in a room in the top of the Lincoln GPO, but in 1940 it moved to St Peter's Chambers, where there was room for offices and rest rooms. The increasing work and decreasing manpower led to the recruitment of Women Observers from 1941, and 1943 saw the Group Operations Room move again, this time to St Martin's Hall, Beaumont Fee. The observer posts were placed at about five mile intervals throughout the county, reporting hostile and friendly aircraft movements to back up the radar system. One observer, J P Kelway, was killed while proceeding to his post at Hackthorn, when his car was attacked and hit by a Dornier Do217, which then crashed. After the war, the Operations Room moved to RAF Waddington, and when the ROC changed its role to nuclear reporting and warning, 15 Group, as Lincoln had become, moved into the first purpose-built underground operations room in the country, on the old Fiskerton airfield.

The Americans

Goxhill, part of the 8th USAAF, continued to receive newly arrived Fighter Groups throughout 1943. These Groups were shipped as an entity from the USA and at Goxhill trained on operational techniques in the British climate. During 1943 came the 78th, 353rd and 356th Fighter Groups, all equipped with the Thunderbolt, each stopping for several months. By the end of 1943 the build up of Groups was virtually complete and the need was for training replacement pilots; thus, in December there came into being the 496th Fighter Training Group (FTG) and this became responsible for the training of pilots destined for the Mustang and Lightning equipped Fighter Groups of both the 8th and newly arrived 9th Air Forces. A second FTG in Shropshire trained the Thunderbolt pilots. 496th FTG left Goxhill in February 1945.

29 *Summer scene at Goxhill, 1944 — Douglas A20B Havoc, 13439, of the USAAF, and possibly of Goxhill station flight.* (P H T Green).

The USAAF in Britain during World War II is popularly thought of as the 8th Air Force's heavy bombers and escort fighters. There was, however, the 9th Tactical Army Air Force, which moved from Italy in late 1943 to support the US Army before, during and after the Invasion. It consisted of fighter bombers, medium bombers and transports, and it was the latter that came to Lincolnshire. The 9th Troop Carrier Command HQ moved into 'St Vincents', Grantham, just vacated by HQ 5 Group Bomber Command, in late 1943. Under its control were 14 Dakota equipped Troop Carrier Groups, split into three Wings, one of which was situated in the West Country, near the 101st US Airborne Division's area, one in Berkshire near the camps of British 6th Airborne, and one in the East Midlands, near the US 82nd Airborne, stationed in Leicestershire, and the British 1st Airborne Division, whose camps lay in east Leicestershire and south Lincs. The RAFs transport force at this time was numerically weak and it was anticipated that the US Dakotas would carry British paratroopers in addition to their own. North Witham was the first airfield taken over by the Americans when, in September 1943, the 1st Tactical Air Depot was established. This unit was the equivalent to an RAF MU, preparing new Dakotas for issue to the operational Groups and performing major maintenance unable to be done at Group level — it was thus a very busy unit, and remained until 1945.

The first Troop Carrier Group to arrive was the 434th at Fulbeck in October 1943; it stayed only until December, when it moved to Aldermaston a new airfield in Berkshire, (now the Atomic Weapons Establishment). Its place was taken by the 442 TCG in March 1944, but this also was a temporary arrangement until Weston Zoyland, its airfield in Somerset, was vacated by the RAF in June. Barkston Heath and Folkingham, however, were chosen to be permament stations under the 52nd Troop Carrier Wing, along with Saltby (Leics), Cottesmore (Rutland) and Spanhoe (Northants), and in February 1944 Barkston received the 61st TCG and Folkingham the 313th. Each unit had 70 Dakotas, C47s as the Americans termed them, divided between four Squadrons, the 61st having the 14th, 15th, 53rd and 59th TCS, and the 313th the 29th, 47th, 48th and 49th.

It was North Witham which became the first Lincolnshire USAAF base to mount an operation when, at 2130 hours on 5 June 1944, the 9th Troop Carrier Command Pathfinder Group C47s started to take off with the pathfinder parachutists for the D-Day drops of the 82nd and 101st Airborne Divisions, dropping them into Normandy just after midnight to set up lights and radar beacons for the main force. Just before midnight on 5 June, the 313th TCG left Folkingham with the 508th Parachute Infantry, 82nd US Airborne, dropping them in Normandy and losing three aircraft, with 21 damaged. The 507th Parachute Infantry boarded the Dakotas of the 442nd Group, Fulbeck, and the 61st, Barkston, which Group despatched three aircraft at a time, at seven second intervals, getting all of its 72 aircraft airborne in five minutes. The 442nd lost two aircraft over Normandy, the 61st one, and the two Groups dropped 1,900 men. The British paratroops involved in D-Day were dropped by RAF aircraft, but for the Arnhem operation the USAAF Groups carried both the British 1st Airborne Division and the US 82nd Airborne Division, flying from Barkston Heath, Folkingham and Fulbeck. Early 1945 saw the 313th and 61st TCG move across to the Continent; Barkston was then taken over by 349th TCG, equipped with C46 Commandos. These aircraft were rarely seen in Europe, and had a reputation for easily catching fire — so much so that the 9th Troop Carrier Command banned them from operations. The 349th left Barkston in April.

30 *A familiar sight at North Witham, Barkston Heath, Folkingham and Fulbeck were the C47 Dakotas of the US 9th Troop Carrier Command. These particular aircraft are from the 434th Troop Carrier Group, possibly at Fulbeck but more likely after their move to Aldermaston.* (USAF).

The reckoning

So the war in Europe ended. Lincolnshire had been the base for almost every type of air warfare — bombing, day and night fighter interception, anti-submarine patrol, shipping strike, flying training, armament training and transport (USAAF). Forty five airfields had been established, having the greatest impact on the landscape since the Enclosure Acts. A rough estimate is that 30,000 acres of the county's land were claimed for use as airfields and this figure was about 1.5% of the total area of the county. Much of this was under concrete, and only now is being reclaimed at some of the airfields, for use as hardcore.The impact on the population was just as great. At a conservative estimate there must have been something like 80,000 RAF personnel stationed in the county. Before the war, Lincolnshire had been a rural county, largely unvisited except for the coast; and yet its own young men were suddenly taken away, to be replaced by other young men (and women) from all parts of Britain and the Commonwealth and from other countries. This cannot have failed to affect the thinking and day-to-day lives of the local people, especially the younger women. Overall, the most noticeable effect must have been noise, from which there would have been little respite. Crashed aircraft were a common sight, sometimes claiming lives and damaging property. Despite all this Lincolnshire people generally made the RAF welcome, although the then LACW Vicki Muhl, stationed at Spilsby and Metheringham, recalls that WAAFs were never asked to people's homes, as were the airmen, and were not liked by the local girls who not unnaturally saw them as competition. WAAFs therefore usually left the camps in groups for company. The Spilsby WAAFs and airmen frequented Skegness, travelling by train from Firsby station. When someone unhooked the guards van one night, LNER took the train off for a few days; which goes to prove that the 'Yellow Bellies' exercised control when necessary!

31 *Lively Lincoln! SX 958 of 9 Sdn gets airborne from Binbrook, in 1950. The Avro Lincoln equipped most of the Lincolnshire bomber squadrons from 1946-1952.* (P H T Green).

32 *A 101 Sdn Lincoln, SX 956, over Cleethorpes, c1950.* (P H T Green).

Part Five

The post war years 1945-1978

The rundown

As after World War I, the end of the war meant rapid demob for many airmen and subsequent disbandment of squadrons and closure of airfields; by the beginning of 1946 only the following were still open for flying — Binbrook, Kirton-in-Lindsey, Manby, Metheringham, North Coates, Scampton, Skellingthorpe, Spilsby, Sturgate, Sutton Bridge, Swinderby and Waddington. The immediate post-war period saw a shuffle round of units as it was decided which to disband and which to retain, a problem also raised for the airfields where the obvious choices for retention were the pre-war Expansion airfields with comfortable, pleasant brick-built accommodation. As far as the squadrons were concerned, the first to be disbanded were those formed during the war, with no other traditions or history — an exception to this was 617 Sdn, which was retained.

As was to be expected, most of the remaining Lincolnshire airfields housed bomber squadrons, as any potential enemy (Russia was already recognised as the threat) would be in northern Europe. Lancasters were still the main equipment but were steadily being replaced by a development, from the same manufacturer, appropriately called the Lincoln. Compared with the Lancaster it was bigger, with a longer range, but with the same bombload and only 10 mph faster. It did, however, have 20 mm cannons instead of the Lancaster's machine guns. The first Lincolns went to 57 Sdn at East Kirkby in August 1945 for use by Tiger Force against Japan, and by 1950 the Lincolnshire bomber squadrons at Binbrook, Waddington and Hemswell were Lincoln equipped, and there were two Mosquito squadrons at Coningsby. 5 Group had disbanded in December 1945 and all of the Lincolnshire bombers were now controlled by 1 Group at Bawtry, again with the exception of Coningsby, which came under 3 Group, Mildenhall. The number of aircraft in each squadron had been drastically reduced to eight, so that it was possible for several squadrons to share one airfield — thus 9, 12, 101 and 617 were at Binbrook, 83 and 97 at Hemswell, 50, 57, 61 and 100 at Waddington and 109 and 139 at Coningsby. The bad winter of 1946/47 curtailed flying at all stations. Binbrook was completely cut off and had supplies dropped by parachute from Transport Command Dakotas.

A Transport Command unit was unique in Lincolnshire, this being 21 Heavy Glider Conversion Unit (HGCU), which brought its Albermarle tugs and Horsa gliders to Elsham Wolds in December 1945, remaining for a year, after which Elsham became non-operational. Metheringham lingered on after the war until 106 Sdn disbanded in February 1946, while Faldingworth continued to operate 300 (Polish) Sdn Lancs until the unit disbanded in October 1946, after which the Mosquito fighter bombers of 305 (Polish) Sdn returned to Faldingworth from Germany, to disband in January 1947. As Poland was by now under Soviet rule many of the Polish airmen settled in Lincolnshire. Faldingworth closed in October 1948. Skellingthorpe housed 58 MU which salvaged crashed aircraft for some years after the war. Spilsby ceased to operate Lancasters in October 1945, but not before it added another Commonwealth country to the list of Lincolnshire-based bomber squadrons, 75 (New Zealand) Sdn, which arrived in July and disbanded in October. Spilsby's proximity to the coastal ranges saw it operate briefly as 2 Armament Practice School, this unit leaving in November 1946. Sturgate also operated Lancasters until 50 and 61 Sdns left in January 1946.

The first jets 1951-1955

The Berlin Airlift highlighted the danger to the West from Russia and the RAF began to grow again, and to re-equip with new aircraft. The tension generated by the Airlift also saw the return of the USAF, and thirty B29s of the 28th Bomb Wing came to Scampton in July 1948. The 301st BW came in October and stopped until February 1949 when, as tension eased, it returned to the States, leaving Scampton to the RAF. Waddington also housed a USAF unit, the 307th BW, and this too was relieved by the 301st, which was split between the two stations. Although Fighter Command was now largely jet equipped with Meteors and Vampires, Bomber Command was still wholly piston engined and the Lincoln was now definitely obsolescent. To boost this meagre force, American aircraft (the first of many), were ordered to equip the heavy bomber squadrons of 3 Group, and in October 1950 149 Sdn flew its Washingtons (as the RAF called the Boeing Superfortress) into Coningsby, followed in 1951 by 15 and 44 Sdns, and in 1952 by 57 Sdn. The Washington, pressurised, comfortable and also operationally better, gave 3 Group the lead over 1 Group but this was not to last long as, in May 1951, 101 Sdn at Binbrook got the RAFs first jet bomber, the Canberra. Although there were several crashes, not unexpectedly in view of the technical advance over previous equipment, the Canberra soon proved a winner, and by 1952 all four Binbrook squadrons were operating Canberras and were joined in August by 50 Sdn. Scampton, which after the war housed 230 OCU — training Lincoln crews for the Command as a whole — and the Bomber Command Instrument Rating and Examining Flight, received four Canberra squadrons in 1953, Nos 10, 27, 18 and 21; Coningsby's Washingtons were replaced by Canberras in 1953, and it was only at Hemswell that the Lincoln soldiered on, with 83 and 97 Sdns, though 109 and 139 also got Canberras in 1953. By 1955, 1 Group had 9 Canberra squadrons, 1 Canberra/Lincoln squadron and 2 Lincoln squadrons. Coningsby had lost its units in 1954.

33 *First English Electric Canberra delivered to an RAF squadron was WD 936, to 101 Sdn at Binbrook on 25 May 1951. The pilot was Roly Beamont (on left of group) chief test pilot for English Electric.* (RAF Binbrook, via P H T Green).

The bomber crew's life in the period from the war to 1955 consisted mainly of training of course, with overseas flights to the many parts of the world still under British sovereignty — in several of these actual operations were undertaken; against the Mau Mau in Kenya, dissident tribesmen in Aden Protectorate and chiefly, against the communist terrorists in Malaya. Each squadron was detached in turn to meet these needs, thus retaining operational experience. With the arrival of the Canberra training intensified and a feature of this was the Lone Ranger flights offered as a reward to crews who had gained a laid down proficiency level in bombing, navigation and general experience. These flights were operated singly to such places as El Adem, Libya; Nicosia, Cyprus; Rhodesia; Germany; Luqa, Malta; Gibraltar; Eastleigh, Kenya; the Canal Zone, Egypt; Khormaksar, Aden and Habbaniyah, Iraq. (The author remembers a Canberra of the Binbrook Wing delivering a sack of Brussels sprouts to Khormaksar — very welcome!). 'Showing the flag' flights were also made, 12 Sdn touring South America and the West Indies during 1952. The squadrons were increased to ten aircraft each, increasing 1 Group's strength impressively.

Training 1945-1955

The Canberra was also issued to Manby which, in 1949, had been renamed the Royal Air Force Flying College. This unit gave selected officers refresher training in all-weather flying, navigation and weapons training. Lincolns were operated too, and a feature of their service was several long distance navigation flights; Aries III, for example, flew a 29,000 miles world trip. The Lincolns, with Valettas, formed 1 Sdn at Manby, while Meteors, Vampires and Athenas (of which the RAFFC had the only examples) were with 2 Sdn at Strubby, reopened in 1949 as Manby's satellite. Later, Hastings transports and Hunter fighters arrived. Manby's Canberras broke several records — Aries IV the London-Capetown in December 1953 and another aircraft the Ottawa-London flight. Aries V set a Transatlantic record, and also one for Tokyo-London.

Mention of the Vampire, Meteor and Hunter jet fighters leads to the observation that, until 1962, no operational fighter squadrons served in Lincolnshire. When Digby's last squadron, 441, left in July 1945, no fighter airfield remained in the county. Digby Sector Ops room, which had moved back to Digby itself, returned to Blankney Hall in September 1945, and in November became Lincolnshire Sector HQ, with its GCI at Langtoft. In March 1946 Lincolnshire Fighter Sector was merged with Yorkshire Fighter Sector, leading to the closure of Blankney Hall in April.

Digby became 1 Officers Advanced Training School, which moved from Cranwell in July 1945. This School trained senior officers for Command and Staff duties, and junior officers for Flight Commander posts. January 1946 saw the airfield used by Tiger Moths of 19 FTS, Cranwell. 1 OATS left in 1947, when the Secretarial Branch Training Establishment and Equipment Officers School moved in. 1948 saw this unit leave, being replaced by Aircrew Educational Unit and Aircrew Transit Unit, they in turn being replaced by 1 Initial Training School, which in 1950 moved to the Isle of Man, making room for 2 ITS. In 1951, flying returned with 2 Grading School, which gave flying training to would-be pilots to assess their suitability for further training. This school was manned by civilian instructors of Airwork Ltd. 2 ITS and 2 GS lasted slightly longer at Digby than the other post war units, but they too left in 1953, when started a period of Care and Maintenance.

1660 HCU at Swinderby continued to train Lancaster crews after the war, though 75 Base disbanded in October 1945. Personnel were trained for a return to civilian life — for example, 3 WAAFs at a time occupied, for one week, a cottage on the WAAF site, and had to budget, shop and cook for themselves — there was no feminist movement in 1945! October and November 1946 saw 1660 move to Lindholme, and its place was taken by 17 OTU from Silverstone, Northants (now the famous motor racing circuit). 17 OTU was equipped with Wellingtons, and operated as the wartime OTUs had done, introducing crews to large, operational aircraft and operational techniques. However, in this immediate post war period the RAF was being re-organised for peacetime efficiency, and in May 1947 the station transferred to Flying Training Command and 17 OTU was retitled 201 Advanced Flying School (AFS), training pilots, navigators and air signallers. Swinderby also housed 21 Group Communications Flight. 202 AFS arrived and amalgamated with 201, and training continued uninterrupted until 1950 when 204 AFS arrived, bringing its Mosquitoes and, once more, overcrowding. Wigsley was re-opened as a satellite. In November F/O Harvey won a George Medal for assisting other members of the crew out of his crashed Wellington, despite his broken back. A year later saw the departure of the Wimpeys and 201 AFS received the RAFs first Varsity crew trainers, 22 being on strength by March 1952. February saw the Mossies of 204 AFS leave for Bassingbourn, leaving the Varsities in sole occupation, and as these were a new type Swinderby hosted the aviation press. It also flew its aircraft around 18 Battle of Britain days in September. Like many other new aircraft, the Varsity had initial problems and was grounded, because of a fault in the tailplane, during the winter. In fact, after several crashes the Varsity had a jinx reputation in the RAF, but by 1954 the problems were overcome and the Varsity was destined to serve the RAF for another 22 years. The unit became 11 FTS in June 1954 and in November air signaller training was transferred to Thorney Island, Hants.

Kirton-in-Lindsey had received 7 Flying Training School, with Oxfords, in April 1946 but this was replaced by 2 ITS, which became 1 Initial Training Wing, training would-be aircrew officers in the basics of RAF life before passing them on to flying training, although their aptitude was tested by very basic training in Tiger Moths.

34 *De Havilland Tiger Moths of 1 Initial Training Wing, Kirton-in-Lindsey, 1952.* (John Walls).

Career officers were still the responsibility of Cranwell. 19 SFTS had replaced 17 SFTS in 1945, but this unit moved to Feltwell, Norfolk, in April 1947, in which month the RAF College was officially re-opened, equipped with Tiger Moths and Harvards. 1 Radio School moved to Somerset in October 1950, followed by 6 Radio School in 1952. From then on Cranwell trained officer cadets only including, from 1955, navigators as well as pilots.

Grantham, having had 17 SFTS transferred in from Cranwell, flew Oxfords until 1947 when the School was renumbered 1 FTS, equipped appropriately enough with the Harvard, which had first seen service at Grantham in 1939. 1 FTS remained until February 1948, having been responsible for training a large Dutch contingent.

North Coates housed a variety of non-flying units such as 1 ITS, 15 School of Technical Training, and also a detachment of search and rescue Sycamore helicopters from 275 Sdn. (Strangely enough, these are the only ASR helicopters to have been based in the county since the war.) Aircraft also came to North Coates for repair and salvage at 54 MU. Of the weapons ranges, Donna Nook closed, but the other three remained open and were used to explode unwanted ammunition after the war's end. Two ammunition MUs lasted until the early 1950s, collecting and disposing of surplus ammunition, but a new unit, 92 MU, took over the bomb storage duties for the Lincolnshire bomber squadrons, being established at Wickenby from 1952 until June 1956.

RAF Hospital Rauceby was required by the civilian authorities and the RAF took over an American military hospital at Nocton Hall in 1947. Many additions were made as time progressed, making the present hospital capable of performing most branches of surgery, medicine and obstetrics. An RAF Nursing School was also established, but disbanded in 1977.

The Korean war had seen US units returning to Europe, and disused airfields all over Britain were designated as reserve USAF airfields, though few saw any active presence — in Lincolnshire these airfields were Blyton, East Kirkby, Sandtoft, Spilsby, Sturgate and Swinderby. During 1954 Sturgate was occupied briefly by the 508 Strategic Fighter Wing with Thunderstreak jet fighters.

The nuclear deterrent

1956 saw the RAFs post war strength reach its peak. The first of the new jet heavy bombers, the V-Bombers, was the Vickers Valiant, which entered RAF service in 1955 but was issued to 3 Group squadrons in Norfolk and Suffolk. The Valiant was actually a 'standby' aircraft, and the first of the really advanced pair of V-Bombers, the Vulcan, was destined for 1 Group. Scampton and Waddington had both been reconstructed in 1954-56, with stronger dispersals and taxiways, specialised buildings, and one long runway which replaced the triangular wartime pattern. Vulcans, of course, carried H-bombs, and special shelters were needed to house these; the storage unit for the bombs was built at Faldingworth to which 92 MU moved, from Wickenby, in 1956-57. 92 MU resembled an American State Penitentiary, surrounded by walls, barbed wire and watch towers with closed circuit TV. These precautions were, of course, very necessary.

The first Vulcans were delivered to the crew training unit, 230 OCU, at Waddington, which was formed in August 1956, displacing two Canberra squadrons, 21 and 27. The OCUs first Vulcan was XA 897 which, proudly displaying Lincoln's coat of arms on its fin, flew to Australia in 23 hours 9 minutes in September 1956. XA 897 flew non-stop from Boscombe Down to Aden in seven hours, presumably the first UK-Aden non-stop flight. Unfortunately, this achievement was marred when XA 897 crashed at London Airport on its return, killing four of the six crew and starting a controversy which has raged ever since regarding the provision of ejector seats for the three rear crew members. Another unfortunate aspect of the accident was that many people thought the flight should have been diverted from the bad weather at London Airport to Waddington, where the weather was much better.

35 *Carrying Lincoln's coat-of-arms on its fin, Avro Vulcan XA 897, first Vulcan delivered to 230 OCU, Waddington, taxis in at Khormaksar, Aden in September 1956 after a seven hour record breaking flight from UK.* (Author).

October 1956 saw the outbreak of the Suez war and the Lincolnshire Canberras were heavily involved in the bombing of Egyptian airfields. 9, 12, 101 and 109 Sdns from Binbrook were based in Malta, while 27 Sdn from Waddington was at Nicosia, Cyprus. The debacle of Suez, diplomatic not military, saw a drastic rethink in defence policy, and thereafter the RAFs strength has progressively reduced. (In 1955 there were 187 operational squadrons, by 1960 - 135, by 1965 - 100, by 1970 - 84 and by 1975 - 69.) The first manifestation of the new defence thinking was the infamous 1957 White Paper in which Duncan Sandys, Minister of Defence, forecast the end of manned aircraft and their replacement by the guided missile. The emphasis was still on the nuclear deterrent, and by the end of 1957, Waddington had its first Vulcan squadron, 83 Sdn. Scampton reopened in 1958, and 617 Sdn reformed with Vulcans in May. Coningsby still operated Canberras, forming 45 Sdn for operations in the Far East and 249 Sdn for service with the Near East Bomber Wing in Cyprus; Binbrook still had three Canberra Squadrons, 9, 12 and 139. Generally, however, the Canberra force was being run down.

The 1957 White Paper's emphasis on missiles saw the delivery to the RAF, in 1958, of the American Thor ICBM, which was to be housed in four complexes along the eastern side of England, each complex with four dispersed sites in addition to a HQ. The HQs were situated at permanent stations, whilst the dispersed sites were on parts of disused wartime airfields. Not unnaturally, Lincolnshire was to house one of the HQs, and Hemswell, whose Canberras had left in 1956, was selected. The missiles were flown in from the USA in Globemaster transports and placed, in squadrons of three missiles each, at the five sites, Hemswell, Bardney, Caistor, Coleby Grange and Ludford. A further site at Folkingham was under the control of the North Luffenham, Rutland, complex. By 1960, all these missiles were in position, and at Scampton 617 and 83 Sdn's Vulcans and Waddington's 44 Sdn provided a large part of the RAFs nuclear strike force, backed up by Coningsby's Canberras of 9 and 12 Sdns. Binbrook's Canberras had left and the station was on Care and Maintenance. To defend the Thor sites and V-bomber airfields, Fighter Command, in addition to its Hunter and Javelin fighters, received squadrons of Bloodhound area defence missiles. Again they were sited mainly on disused wartime airfields, but the first station to be equipped with the Bloodhound and its associated radar tracking sets was North Coates, where in April 1958 264 Sdn reformed. Other Bloodhound sites in the County were Dunholme Lodge (141 Sdn) and Woodhall Spa (112 Sdn), each site having 16 missiles. Wing HQs for Bloodhounds were at Grantham and Kirton-in-Lindsey.

1960 saw the end of National Service and the return to a wholly professional RAF. During the early 1960s the V-force continued to expand, the Vulcan B2 entering service during 1960, when 83 Sdn, Waddington, replaced its Mark 1s. The B2 was a vastly improved version, designed to carry the Blue Steel stand-off bomb which came into use at Scampton with 617 Sdn in February 1963. The Cuba crisis in 1962 saw the V and Thor Forces at operational readiness but by 1963 the Thor's vulnerability to air attack was evident and the Thor force disbanded. Hemswell was used for recruit training until 1967 when it went on to Care and Maintenance. 1965 saw Waddington's Vulcan wing comprising 44, 50 and 101 Sdns and these have remained ever since. Scampton wing was 27, 83 and 617 Sdns while a third Lincolnshire wing, at Coningsby, of 9, 12 and 35 Sdns, had operated from 1962 until November 1964, when it moved to Cottesmore, Rutland. At this time the V-bombers were a highly professional force, with training at a very high pitch and a destructive power far outweighing that of the World War II Lancaster force. 27 Sdn had reformed at Scampton on 1 April 1964, on Vulcan B2s, and, like the Canberra days, emphasis was placed on 'global mobility', involving Lone Ranger flights to many parts of the world, including Strategic Air Command bases in the USA. This became such a regular feature that Goose Bay airfield, Labrador, became a sub-station of Waddington, and remains so today. Visits to Australia were fairly common and air displays all over the world asked for Vulcan participation. The squadrons also took part in the annual Strategic Air Command bombing competition. 1963 saw the end of Squadron groundcrew, as 'centralised servicing' was deemed to be more economic and efficient. All aircraft were allocated to a station and only the aircrew belonged to a Squadron, a fact much regretted by all concerned as Squadron *esprit de corps* had played a very large part in RAF tradition. In fact, the old system returned in the early 1970s.

36 *Avro Vulcan B2, XL 446, of 35 Sdn, Scampton, shows off its low-level camouflage scheme, first applied to the V-bombers in 1969.* (P H T Green).

Coningsby had closed to be reconstructed to operate the new Canberra replacement, the TSR 2. Despite the promise showed by this aircraft in its first test flights, the incoming Labour Government of 1965 cancelled it and several other new aircraft destined for the RAF, thus ensuring that for twenty years the RAF would not operate truly modern bomber aircraft comparable with those in service in the USA and, more importantly, Russia and its satellite countries. The aircraft ordered to fill in for the TSR 2, the American F111, was also cancelled, as was the Anglo-French Variable Geometry aircraft ordered to replace the F111. The final 'replacement' aircraft, the Tornado, is intended to be stationed in Lincolnshire in 1980 or thereabouts, years after the TSR 2 would have been in service, and at a cost of millions of pounds in cancellation charges paid out on the previous aircraft. Bomber Command disappeared on 1 April 1968 and the Vulcans then came under 1 (Bomber) Group, Strike Command. The Blue Steels were withdrawn in 1969 and the intended replacement, Skybolt, cancelled by the Americans.

So, 22 years after it first entered service, the Vulcan soldiers on in a low flying role for which it was not designed. Its electronics and other systems have been updated and its nuclear role was handed over to the Royal Navy's Polaris submarines in 1969. 92 MU, Faldingworth, no longer needed for nuclear storage, closed in November 1972. The Vulcan force in Lincolnshire has altered little over the past decade, 83 Sdn disbanding at Scampton in July 1969, its place being taken by 230 OCU. The OCU flew, apart from its Vulcans, the RAFs last four Hastings — affectionately known as '1066 Squadron' — used as radar trainers. Towards the end of their service life they were also used for patrol of North Sea oil production platforms, eventually retiring from service in 1977. 27 Sdn was disbanded in March 1972, but reformed a year later with the strategic-reconnaissance version of the Vulcan, the only squadron to operate this variant. In January 1975 two further Vulcan squadrons arrived, due to the evacuation of Cyprus where they had been based. 9 Sdn came to Waddington, and 35 to Scampton. Thus, at the time of writing, all the RAFs Vulcans are Lincolnshire based, 9, 44, 50 and 101 Sdns at Waddington, 27, 35, 617 Sdns and 230 OCU at Scampton. 617 Sdn is reported as likely to be the first Tornado unit in the early 1980s.

37 *Hastings T5, TG517, of '1066 Sdn' 230 OCU finally retired from service in 1977. Reminiscent of the bomb log carried by many WWII aircraft, 517 sports four codfish below the cockpit, battle honours gained on Icelandic 'cod war' patrols which were flown from Scampton.* (Middleton, Lincoln).

Air defence 1955-1978

The Bloodhound 1 missile sites closed down in the mid sixties, except at North Coates. 264 Sdn disbanded in 1962, but 17 Joint Services Trials Unit arrived to introduce into service the Bloodhound Mark 2, and in October 1963 25 Sdn formed up on these new, improved missiles, remaining at North Coates until it moved to Germany in February 1971. North Coates then began to run down.

Lincolnshire was not now without fighter protection however as Binbrook had been taken over by Fighter Command in April 1960. It remained on Care and Maintenance until June 1962, when 64 Sdn arrived with its Javelin delta-wing all-weather fighters. The Javelin was then the standard equipment of the all-weather squadrons, and 64 Sdn was joined by the Central Fighter Establishment in October. The CFEs task was to work out the RAFs fighter tactics, and to tie these in to the new types of aircraft — it was thus equipped with Hunters, Javelins and Lightnings. A third unit, arriving in May 1963, was 85 Sdn, equipped with Canberras and Meteors, its task being to tow targets for air-to-air firing by fighter squadrons and to provide high speed radar targets against which fighters and radar stations could practice interceptions. These three units operated together until 64 Sdn left for Singapore in April 1965.

100

The Javelin replacement, the much more potent Lightning, arrived with 5 Sdn in October. The Lightning was the RAFs first supersonic jet fighter, and 5 Sdn was one of the oldest RAF squadrons, having served for most of its history in India, until it reformed in Germany in 1952, from where it came to Binbrook. It celebrated its Golden Jubilee on 25 November 1966. 5 Sdn Lightnings were the F6, the latest version. The CFE disbanded on 1 February 1966, but a component part, the Air Fighting Development Squadron, was renamed the Fighter Command Trials Unit and continued to serve at Binbrook with Lightnings until it disbanded in June 1967. Fighter Command became 11 (Fighter) Group, Strike Command, on 1 April 1968, and Binbrook was one of its few fighter stations, the others being Leuchars, Fifeshire, and Wattisham, Suffolk. 85 Sdn Canberras left for Norfolk in January 1972, and Binbrook became an all Lightning base when 11 Sdn moved in from Leuchars in March. 11 had also served in the Far and Middle East, and Germany. Both squadrons are part of the UK Air Defence Force, tasked with the interception of unidentified aircraft picked up by UK radar. They occasionally made overseas trips to Malta for armament training,

38 *As Canberras were retired from bombing duties they were given many non-operational roles. WD948 of 85 Sdn, Binbrook, provided target facilities for the station's fighters. In the background can be seen the radar nose of one of the Squadron's Canberra T11s. (P H T Green).*

but the final trip was made by 11 Sdn in 1978. Detachments are also made to Valley, Anglesey, for training in missile firing, and the two squadrons compete each year to provide a solo display pilot. More seriously, Binbrook has two Lightnings on twenty-four hour Quick Reaction Alert which are scrambled to identify any unscheduled radar plots. Lightning pilots are a mixture of experienced and first tour airmen, and average about twenty five sorties per month. Binbrook will be the last station to operate an all-British interceptor, the two Lightning squadrons expecting to remain operational until 1984/5, and to provide trained pilots until then Binbrook operates the Lightning Training Flight with two seat T5s.

39 *No 11 Sdn brought its BAC Lightnings to Binbrook in 1972. F6, XR 757, is seen in the natural metal finish originally sported by all RAF Lightnings. (P H T Green).*

Coningsby, after its vicissitudes with TSR2, was elected as the first base for the Phantom fighter-bomber, which had been ordered from the USA to help fill the gap left by the cancellation of the TSR2. The Phantom was re-engined with Rolls-Royce Spey engines, and Coningsby first received 5 School of Technical Training to train groundcrew personnel. In February 1968, under 38 Group, Air Support Command, 228 OCU formed to train the Phantom aircrews in the ground attack and tactical reconnaissance roles for the UK and Germany based squadrons. The first operational unit, 6 Sdn, formed in May 1969, followed by 54 Sdn in September and the two squadrons and the OCU made Coningsby a very busy airfield. A third unit, 41 Sdn, formed in April 1972, specifically for the tactical reconnaissance role. Overseas detachments to Cyprus and Sardinia, for armament training, were regular events, and both Coningsby and Binbrook had many exchange visits with other NATO airforces. 1974 saw a change of role, when the Jaguar began to take over the ground attack and reconnaissance role, and the Phantom replaced the Lightning on air defence. 6 and 54 Sdns disbanded in June and March 1974 respectively, though 41 remained until 1977, and the station transferred to 11 (Fighter) Group. 228 OCU now trains Phantom crews for air defence work and the Lightning squadrons came to Coningsby to convert to Phantoms. 111 was the first, in October 1974, followed by 29 which became the resident squadron on air defence duties, the

40 *A 29 Sdn Phantom crew returns to Coningsby from a practice mission, 1977.* (RAF Coningsby).

Phantom's longer range and two man crew enabling it to provide cover further afield than the Binbrook Lightnings. 111 left in November 1975, 23 formed in October 1975, followed by 56 in March 1976. Also in March 1976 much older equipment touched down at Coningsby — the Hurricanes, Spitfires and Lancaster of the Battle of Britain Flight. Woodhall Spa is an out-station used for engine testing.

A third 11 Group station in the county came with the re-activation of North Coates. At last the seriously low state of Britain's air defences had been partially recognised by the Government, and 85 Sdn reformed at West Raynham, Norfolk, as a Bloodhound 2 missile site, the missiles themselves being withdrawn from Singapore and Cyprus. B Flight of 85 Sdn was set up at North Coates in 1976.

Theddlethorpe, Holbeach and Wainfleet ranges continued to provide range facilities both for the Lincolnshire units and the rest of the UK-based RAF and USAF squadrons, not to mention other NATO air forces. Complaints over noise and the occasional accidental dropping of a bomb mean the ranges are extremely concerned about relations with local communities. Theddlethorpe, near several villages, closed in December 1973, when Donna Nook was reopened, becoming operational in August 1976. Flying is kept as far as possible to the seaward side of the seabank at all the ranges and the beaches at Donna Nook cleared of all debris each Friday. Practice weapons only are used, all bombs, rockets and cannon shells being inert except for a smoke and flash compound which enables their impact to be accurately plotted and scored. Most attacks are made below 500 feet, and at Donna Nook these can be watched from the Stonebridge car park; as the CO says, 'We are proud of the fact that we have became a tourist attraction!'.

Training 1955-1978

The RAF College, in 1955, still operated the piston engined Prentice, Chipmunk and Balliol, with Valettas and Varsities for navigator training. Tarmac runways were laid on the south airfield by 1954 and Vampires and Meteors began to arrive. Barkston Heath and Fulbeck were taken into use as relief airfields, Fulbeck having stored several German World War II aircraft of the Air Historical Branch after the war, and by 1961 the pilots trained from the start on Jet Provosts. Much new building took place, and the last of the World War I wooden huts disappeared in 1960. 1966 saw the arrival of the RAF Technical College from Henlow, and this merged with the RAF College, using the new Trenchard Hall.

Another change took place when the system of entry altered — entrants now attend University, serving with the University Air Squadrons before coming to Cranwell to receive basic RAF training, and pilot training for those wanting to be aircrew. All career officers, of any Branch, now train initially at Cranwell and, of course, officers come also from many overseas countries. The term cadet has disappeared, as entrants are now acting P/O. Close links are maintained with the French Air Force and US Air Force sister academies, involving exchange visits. There are facilities for many sports and interests. An aerobatics team, 'The Poachers', has been formed and attends many air displays each season, its mount being the Jet Provost T5. Fulbeck closed in the late 1960s but Barkston remains as a relief airfield.

41 *The current Lincolnshire aerobatic team is 'The Poachers' from Cranwell, whose Jet Provost T5s are seen here over the magnificent College building.* (RAF Cranwell, via P H T Green).

Lincolnshire's other college, the RAF Flying College, became well established at Manby and Strubby. In 1958, 4 Sdn was formed with Provosts of the Refresher Flight. Hunters and Lincolns had gone by 1961 and Jet Provosts replaced the piston engined Varsity in 1964 with the School of Refresher Flying, which had become a separate unit when the College was renamed the RAF College of Air Warfare. Manby became increasingly civilianised, as Airwork Services Limited took over some airmen's duties, and the last WRAF left in 1965. Another departure in that year was the last Meteor, and the last Canberra left in 1966, Manby being the first station to receive the new Dominie crew trainer. The College ran courses in electronic warfare, aerosystems etc, and the School of Refresher Flying retrained aircrew who had been doing ground jobs for some time. The CAW now operated Jet Provosts, some of which formed the Macaws aerobatic team. Strubby closed in September 1972, due to the poor state of the runways, and in December 1973 the CAW, vicitim of more Defence cuts, moved to Cranwell to merge with the RAF College, becoming the Department of Air Warfare. The School of Refresher Flying moved to Leeming in Yorkshire, and in March 1974 Manby closed, causing considerable hardship in the surrounding area.

Cranwell received yet further lodgers when Little Rissington airfield closed, causing the Central Flying School, whose base it was, to disperse to several airfields. The HQ of the CFS, plus its Jet Provost Squadron, which trains Jet Provost instructors, moved to Cranwell in April 1976 but such were the disadvantages of the dispersed CFS that November 1977 saw the CFS elements leave Cranwell for Leeming. The Department of Air Warfare Dominies also left Cranwell in 1977, leaving the College operating only the Jet Provost.

The county's third flying training base, Swinderby, saw changes in 1955. 11 FTS left for Hampshire in June, and was replaced by 8 FTS. Whereas 11 FTS had trained bomber crews, 8 FTS was solely a pilot training establishment, equipped with Vampire T11s. New buildings sprang up, including a control tower, and trees at the end of the runway were felled. The station now came under 25 Group, and Morton Hall, formerly HQ of 21 Group, closed. 8 FTS operated 17 T11s and FB5s, with a student population of 120, courses starting at nine week intervals; the students had already completed Provost basic training and some, recalling the (P)AFUs, were acclimatized to British methods after training in Canada. FAA and foreign pilots were included. An experimental change in methods came when 8 Provosts arrived, and all-through training was initiated, students moving on to the Vampire for jet training. The all-through experiment concluded, apparently a failure, and the Provosts left Swinderby. Two Vampire aerobatic teams were formed and did tours of the Battle of Britain displays. Wigsley, which had been reopened as a satellite, closed again in 1958, and Winthorpe was used as Swinderby's satellite, but it also closed in 1959. After threat of closure, the delay in the introduction into service of the Gnat gave 8 FTS a reprieve, and Swinderby became extremely busy. However, the reprieve was only temporary and in March 1964 8 FTS disbanded, and flying at Swinderby ceased due to the nearness of Waddington and Cranwell circuits.

The station now came under Technical Training Command and, in June, 7 School of Recruit Training opened when its first intake arrived, further intakes arriving in eight weekly cycles. A shortage of accommodation sent 2 Wing to Hemswell during the winter, remaining there until May 1967. July 1970 saw the number 7 disappear from the school's title, and it became the RAF School of Recruit Training, the only School of its type in the RAF, and it has remained so ever since, all airmen entering the RAF through Swinderby. At the time of writing, the School trains 6,000-7,000 recruits a year. Each course arrives on a Wednesday and is kitted out etc for three days. Then follows ten days of drill and lectures on Service knowledge. Two weeks of security and general defence training by the RAF Regiment are followed by three days Tented Field Training in Sherwood Forest. Then follows more drill, PT, and lectures, making a six week course before the passing out parade on a Wednesday. As can be seen, drill takes third place to PT (40 periods) and security training in the modern RAF. Occasional flying still takes place; for example, East Midlands University Air Sdn and 7 Air Experience Flight operated from Swinderby during 1977 because of the bad grass surface at Newton.

Digby became a communications base in 1955 with the arrival of 399 Signals Unit in January, this being joined by 591 SU in July. Wireless masts sprang up all over the old airfield and, in September 1959, the Wireless Operators School and Aerial Erectors School arrived. The Wireless Operators School moved to North Luffenham in 1964, but the two SUs remained, being joined by a third unit, 54 SU from the Far East, in 1967. The work of Digby is obviously secret, so there is little more to say about the station except that it is one of the oldest RAF stations to have been in continual use.

Grantham, also an old station, ceased flying with the departure of 1 FTS in 1948. Now under Technical Training Command, the RAF Officer Cadet Training Unit arrived in March 1948, remaining until March 1954. Various non-flying units were based there, the Mess Staff School, 1949-57; HQ 24 Group, Technical Training Command, 1954-57; the School of Education, 1955-58; RAF Central Library 1955-58; Secretarial

Officers School, 1959; HQ 3 RAF Police District, 1959, later renamed HQ Provost and Security Services. In December 1961 the WRAF Depot moved in and all airwomen did their basic training here until the Depot moved to Hereford in March 1974. The Central Gliding School remained until 1975, after which the Royal Corps of Transport took over the station.

Kirton-in-Lindsey, like Grantham and Digby, ceased to be used for powered flying because of its grass surface. 1960 saw the arrival of 7 School of Technical Training and it also became 2 Gliding Centre. 7 School of Technical Training left in 1965, and on 3 December, Kirton transferred to the Royal Artillery, housing Light Anti-Aircraft Regiments. Flying of a sort still takes place, as these Regiments now operate the Rapier anit-aircraft missile, and Army Air Corps helicopters sometimes drop in.

And so this story of 60 years of the RAF in Lincolnshire ends. The units now here, in July 1978, are 9, 44, 50 and 101 Vulcan Squadrons at Waddington; 27, 35, 617 Sdns, and 230 OCU, with Vulcans, at Scampton; 5 and 11 Sdns with Lightnings and the Lightning Training Flight at Binbrook; 29 Sdn and 228 OCU Phantoms, and the Battle of Britain Flight, at Coningsby; RAF College, Jet Provosts, Cranwell; RAF School of Recruit Training, Swinderby; RAF Hospital, Nocton Hall; 54, 399, 591 Signals Units, Aerial Erectors School, Digby; Air Weapons Ranges, Donna Nook, Wainfleet and Holbeach; B Flight, 85 Sdn, Bloodhound SAM2s, North Coates.

Full details of developments from 1978 to 1985 can be found in 'Bomber County 2', published by Lincolnshire Recreational Services – Libraries in 1985, which also gives additional information on the years 1912-1978 with completely different photos. These brief notes to the 5th impression of the original 'Bomber County' are intended to bring the reader up-to-date with RAF developments in the county of Lincolnshire for the years 1978 to mid-1989.

BARKSTON HEATH. Still continues as a relief landing ground for Cranwell but in 1983 a Bloodhound SAM 2 air defence missile squadron was formed at Wyton, Cambs, and its A Flight was based at a new complex on the north side of Barkston Heath. This squadron was 25 Squadron until 1989, when the number was handed over to a new Tornado fighter unit at Leeming, and at the time of writing the new number was yet to be decided.

BINBROOK. With the run-down of the Lightning force, the Lightning Training Flight was the first Binbrook unit to disband, in April 1987. 5 Squadron also disbanded, in December of that year, moving to Coningsby and Tornados. 11 Squadron soldiered on as the last Lightning (and all-British fighter?) unit until April 1988 when it too disbanded. Binbrook as an RAF station then closed, though its runways are still used by aircraft from the CFS at Scampton.

CONINGSBY. The Phantoms of 28 Sdn and 228 OCU continued to keep Coningsby busy until 229 OCU, with the new Panavia Tornado F2, formed in May 1985 to train crews for the RAF's latest fighter. Hardened Aircraft Shelters had been built to house the new aircraft and the first operational unit, 29 Sdn, converted from the Phantom in April 1987 to the latest version, the Tornado F3, which also was then used by the OCU. This left no room for 228 OCU and its Phantoms, which moved to Leuchars in the same month severing an 18 year link between Coningsby and the Phantom. The station received its full complement of flying units when a second operational squadron, No5, joined 29 and 229 OCU in January 1988.

42   *The RAFs last flying Lancaster, PA 474 of the Battle of Britain Memorial Flight, Coningsby, over Lincoln in 1976. Named 'City of Lincoln' in recognition of the close ties between the RAF and the City.*

43 *Lightning F6, XR 755, of 5 Sdn Binbrook.* (P H T Green).

CRANWELL. In August 1979 the RAF College ceased to be a flying training unit, concentrating on its officer training role which now embraced all officers, men and women, regardless of their intended length of service or trade. The flying unit became the Basic Flying Training School, completely separate from the College. In February 1989 this title was brought into line with the other FTSs by renaming it No.3 FTS, a unit with a long history including service at Grantham in the 1920s and 30s. 3 FTS will lose its faithful Jet Provost T5s in the early 1990s as, on present plans, it becomes the last school to receive the RAF's new basic trainer, the Short Tucano T1.

DIGBY. No change.

NOCTON HALL. The RAF Hospital closed in March 1983. Now a USAF Reserve Hospital.

NORTH COATES. No change.

SCAMPTON. The Scampton Vulcan Wing started to run down in 1981 when 230 OCU disbanded, followed by 617 Sdn (January 1982), 35 Sdn (February 1982) and 27 Sdn (March 1982). The station was then without flying units until March of the following year, when the RAF Aerobatic Team, 'The Red Arrows', and their Hawk T1 aircraft arrived. 'The Arrows' were joined by the Central Flying School, of which they are a part, in September 1984. The CFS HQ, and its Jet Provost and Bulldog Squadrons, are now well established at Scampton and train the flying instructors for these types. The first Short Tucano T1, the RAF's new trainer, arrived in 1988 and the CFS is currently establishing the training course on this aircraft, which will then replace the Jet Provost.

Whilst the Vulcans were still in service, 2503 (County of Lincoln) Squadron, Royal Auxilliary Air Force Regiment, was formed at Scampton in July 1979. The task of its 'weekend airmen' was to guard the station against attack from saboteurs or enemy ground forces. In February 1985, the Vulcans having gone, 2503 Sdn moved to Waddington.

SWINDERBY. The School of Recruit Training took over the training of WRAF recruits as well as airmen in October 1982. Flying returned to the station in July 1979, when the Flying Selection Squadron was formed, with Chipmunk T10s, to give prospective pilots who had no flying experience a 14 hour flying programme which would assess their flying aptitude. This saved the RAF a substantial sum of money by cutting out those without aptitude at an early stage and the FSS became the Elementary Flying Training Squadron in June 1987, running a 65 hour basic training course.

WADDINGTON. As at Scampton the Vulcan squadrons began to disband in 1982, with 9 Sdn being the first, in May. However, the Falklands war saw the process halted and the Vulcans used in anger for the first time. With the war won, 101 Sdn disbanded in August 1982, and 44 Sdn in December. 50 Sdn survived until March 1984 because its Vulcans were converted into tankers, as the B2(K), to overcome the RAF's shortage of such aircraft until the VC 10 K2 entered service at Brize Norton. Waddington then played host to the ill-fated Nimrod AEW3 programme until its cancellation in 1985. The station was named as the base for the Nimrod's replacement, the Boeing Sentry AEW1, but this is not destined to enter service, with 8 Squadron, until 1991. In the meantime Waddington has acted as a 'spare' airfield, its most notable use being that as the venue for the 1986 NATO Fighter Meet.

2503 (County of Lincoln) Sdn (R.Aux.A.F.) arrived in February 1985 to guard the AEWs, and were joined by 2729 (City of Lincoln) Sdn in April, with its captured Argentinian 30mm anti-aircraft guns. 2729's job is to protect Waddington and its invaluable future aircraft from air attack, and it is also manned by part-time airmen and women.

DONNA NOOK, HOLBEACH and WAINFLEET continue as Air Weapon Ranges.

Thus, Lincolnshire is no longer 'Bomber County'; its based units are either for air-defence or for training, much as they were in 1918 when the RAF formed.

Part Six

Where were they?

Lincolnshire RAF stations, showing major units housed at each, and Ordnance Survey National Grid reference (1 : 50,000 series). Bracketed dates after aircraft name denotes year of re-equipment with that type.

ANWICK. Sheet 121 NGR 110510. WWI emergency landing ground.

BARDNEY. Sheet 121 NGR 132706. Opened April 1943. 9 Sdn, Lancaster, April 1943 - July 1945. 189 Sdn, Lancaster, formed October 1944 - November 1944. Closed 1945. Reopened 1959, 106 Sdn, Thor ICBM, 1959 - disb 1963. Closed 1963.

BARKSTON HEATH. Sheet 130 NGR 960410. Opened April 1941. Relief landing ground for Cranwell until April 1943. Runways laid. Reopened January 1944. USAAF 9th AF 61st TCG, Dakota, February 1944 - March 1945. 349th TCG Commando. March 1945 - April 1945. RAF non-flying April 1945 - closed. Reopened as relief landing ground for Cranwell, 1954? to present. Still open.

BELTON PARK. Sheet 130 NGR 930380. Opened December 1941, RAF Regt depot, December 1941 - August 1946. Closed August 1946.

BINBROOK. Sheet 113 NGR 186956. Opened June 1940. 12 Sdn, Battle/Wellington, July 1940 - August 1940, September 1940 - September 1942. 142 Sdn, Battle/Wellington, July 1940 - August 1940, September 1940 - November 1941. 1 Group Target Towing Flight (TTF) Lysander, September 1941 - November 1941 renamed 1481 TTF November 1941 - ? Closed September 1942 - May 1943 for runway construction. 460 Sdn, Lancaster, May 1943 - July 1945. 12 Sdn, Lancaster, Lincoln (1946) September 1945 - November 1947. 101 Sdn, Lancaster, Lincoln (1946), Canberra (1951), October 1945 - disb February 1957. 9 Sdn, Lancaster/Lincoln, April 1946 - August 1951. 617 Sdn, Lincoln, May 1946 - July 1947, Lincoln, Canberra (1952), September 1947 - disb December 1955. 50 Sdn, Lincoln, August 1947 - December 1947. 12 Sdn, Lincoln, Canberra (1952), March 1948 - October 1955. 9 Sdn, Canberra, October 1951 - March 1956, June 1956 - June 1959. 50 Sdn, Canberra, August 1952 - January 1956. 139 Sdn, Canberra, January 1956 - disb December 1959.

109 Sdn, Canberra, January 1956 - disb February 1957. 12 Sdn, Canberra, March 1956 - September 1956, December 1956 - July 1959. Care and Maintenance. Central Fighter Est. October 1962 - disb February 1966. 64 Sdn, Javelin, June 1962 - April 1965. 85 Sdn, Canberra & Meteor, April 1963 - February 1972. 5 Sdn, Lightning, reformed October 1965 - present. Air Fighting Dev Sdn, February 1966, renamed Fighter Command Trials Unit, disb June 1967. 11 Sdn, Lightning, March 1972 - present. Lightning Conversion Unit, formed September 1974, renamed Lightning Training Flight - present. Still open.

BLANKNEY HALL. Sheet 121 NGR 068600. Opened 1940? Digby Sector Ops room, 1940 - 1945. Closed. Reopened September 1945. Digby Sector Ops room, September 1945, renamed Lincolnshire Sector HQ, November 1945 - March 1946. Closed April 1946.

BLYTON. Sheet 112 NGR 865952. Opened November 1942. 199 Sdn, Wellington, formed November 1942 - February 1943. 1662 Heavy Conversion Unit, Halifax and Stirling, formed February 1943 - 1945. Closed 1945.

BRACEBRIDGE HEATH. Sheet 121 NGR 985673. Opened 1919, 4 AAP, 1919 - disb 1920. 120 Sdn, 1919 disb 1919. Closed 1920.

BRACEBY. Sheet 130 NGR 015355. WWI emergency landing ground.

44 *World War I hangars still in situ at Bracebridge Heath, 1978. Currently used as warehousing by E H Lee.* (Lincolnshire Library Service).

113

BRATTLEBY See SCAMPTON.

BUCKMINSTER. Sheet 130 NGR 893235. Opened September 1916, One flight 38 Sdn, FE2, September 1916 - May 1918. 90 Sdn, Dolphin & Avro 504 NF, reformed August 1918 - disb June 1919. Aircraft Acceptance Park, 1918-1919. Closed 1919.

BUCKNALL. Sheet 121 NGR 170690. WWI emergency landing ground.

CAISTOR. Sheet 112 NGR 081017. Opened 1941. Relief landing ground for Kirton-in-Lindsey. December 1942, RLG for Manby. May 1943, RLG for Kirton-in-Lindsey. 1944 RLG for Cranwell. Closed 1945. Reopened 1960, 269 Sdn, Thor ICBM, 1960 - disb 1963. Closed 1963.

CAMMERINGHAM. See INGHAM.

COCKTHORNE. Sheet 121 NGR 070875. WWI emergency landing ground.

COLEBY GRANGE. Sheet 121 NGR 000600. Opened 1940. 1940 RLG for Cranwell. 1941 RLG for Waddington. 409 Sdn, Defiant/Beaufighter, July 1941 - February 1943. 410 Sdn, Mosquito, February 1943 - October 1943. 288 Sdn, Blenheim, March 1943 - November 1943. 264 Sdn, Mosquito, November 1943 - December 1943. 68 Sdn, Mosquito, February 1944 - March 1944. 307 Sdn, Mosquito, March 1944 - May 1944. Closed. Reopened 1959. 142 Sdn, Thor ICBM, 1959 - disb 1963. Closed 1963.

CONINGSBY. Sheet 122 NGR 216562. Opened November 1940. 106 Sdn, Hampden, Manchester/Lancaster (1942), February 1941 - September 1942. 97 Sdn, Manchester/Lancaster (1942), March 1941 - August 1942. 5 Group TTF, Lysander, September 1941 - November 1941. 1514 Beam Approach Training Flight, Oxford, November 1941 - ? Runways laid September 1942 - August 1943. 617 Sdn, Lancaster, August 1943 - January 1944. 619 Sdn, Lancaster, January 1944 - April 1944. 61 Sdn, Lancaster, February 1944 - April 1944. 83 Sdn, Lancaster, April 1944 - October 1946. 97 Sdn, Lancaster, April 1944 - November 1946. 109 Sdn, Mosquito, November 1946 - March 1950. 139 Sdn, Mosquito, November 1946 - April 1950. 231 OCU, Mosquito, 1947. 149 Sdn, Washington, Canberra (1953), October 1950 - May 1954. 15 Sdn, Washington, Canberra (1953), February 1951 - May 1954. 44 Sdn, Washington, Canberra (1953), May 1951 - May 1954. 57 Sdn, Washington, Canberra (1953), April 1952 - May 1954. 40 Sdn, Canberra, formed October 1953 - February 1954. Care and Maintenance. 57 Sdn, Canberra, November 1956 - disb December 1957. 249 Sdn, Canberra, formed August 1957 - October 1957. 45 Sdn, Canberra, November 1957 - December 1957. Care and Maintenance. 12 Sdn, Canberra, July 1959 - disb July 1961. 9 Sdn, Canberra, August 1959 - disb July 1961. Rebuilding. 9 Sdn, Vulcan, formed March 1962 - November 1964. 12 Sdn, Vulcan, formed July 1962 - November 1964. 35 Sdn, Vulcan, formed December 1962 - November 1964. Rebuilt for TSR2. 228 OCU, Phantom, formed February 1968 - present. 6 Sdn, Phantom, formed May 1969 - disb June 1974. 54 Sdn, Phantom, formed September 1969 - disb March 1974. 41 Sdn, Phantom, formed April 1972 - 1977. 111 Sdn, Phantom, formed October 1974 - November 1975. 29 Sdn, Phantom, formed December 1974 - present. 23 Sdn, Phantom, formed October 1975 - February 1976. 56 Sdn, Phantom, formed March 1976 - July 1976. Battle of Britain Flight, March 1976 - present. Still open.

CRANWELL. Sheet 130 NGR 000490. Opened April 1916. RN Aeroplane, Airship and Balloon training station, HMS Daedalus - April 1918. 201 TDS, renamed 56 TDS, April 1918 - 1919. 202 TDS renamed 57 TDS, April 1918 - 1919. 213 TDS renamed 58 TDS, April 1918 - 1919. HQ 59th Training Wing 1918 - 1919. Airship Training Wing 1918 - 1919. Boys Training Wing 1918 - 1919. Wing Aeroplane Repair Section 1918 - 1919. Electrical and Wireless School, renamed Wireless Operators School, 1916 - June 1918. RAF Cadet College, February 1920 - renamed RAF College 1929 to September 1939. 1 Signals School, 1920 - 1943, renamed 1 Radio School - 1950. Apprentice School 1920 - 1926. RAF Hospital 1922 - 1940. School of Store Accountancy and Storekeeping, July 1934 - December 1936, renamed Equipment Training School - June 1941. Supplies Depot, October 1936 - November 1949. School of Clerks Accountancy 1939 - 1941. RAF College SFTS, August 1939 - March 1944, renamed 17 SFTS March 1944 - May 1945. HQ 21 Group, December 1939 - July 1944. 2 FIS, formed July 1940, renamed 2 CFS - June 1941. 8 RS, 1941 - 1945. 3 OTU, August 1941 - June 1943. 19 SFTS, renamed 19 FTS, June 1945 - April 1947. RAF College, April 1947 - present. 3 Initial Training Wing, January 1951 - March 1953. Central Flying School HQ and Jet Provost Squadron, April 1976 - November 1977. Still open.

CUXWOLD. Sheet 113 NGR 177008. WWI emergency landing ground.

DIGBY. Sheet 121 NGR 038565. Opened September 1918, originally called SCOPWICK. 59 TDS, September 1918 - December 1918, renamed 59 Training Sdn, December 1918 - September 1919. 203 Sdn, Camel, December 1919 - disb January 1920. 11 Sdn, F2b, September 1919 - disb December 1919. 25 Sdn, F2b, 1919 - disb January 1920. 209 Sdn, Camel, February 1919 - disb June 1919. 210 Sdn, Camel, February 1919 - disb June 1919. 213 Sdn, Camel, March 1919 - disb December 1919. 3 FTS, April 1920 - April 1922. 2 FTS, June 1924 - disb December 1933, reformed October 1934 - September 1937. 46 Sdn, Gauntlet, Gladiator (1938), Hurricane (1939), November 1937 - November 1939. 73 Sdn, Gladiator, Hurricane (1939), November 1937 - September 1939. 504 Sdn, Hurricane, September 1939 - October 1939. 229 Sdn, Blenheim 1F, October 1939 - June 1940. 611 Sdn, Spitfire, October 1939 - July 1940. 46 Sdn, Hurricane, January 1940 - May 1940. 111 Sdn, Hurricane, May 1940. 222 Sdn, Blenheim 1F/Spitfire, May 1940. 56 Sdn, Hurricane, May 1940 - June 1940. 79 Sdn, Hurricane, May 1940 - June 1940. 46 Sdn, Hurricane, June 1940 - September 1940. 29 Sdn, Blenheim 1F, June 1940 - April 1941. 151 Sdn, Hurricane, September 1940 - November 1940. 46 Sdn, Hurricane, December 1940 - February 1941. 402 Sdn, Hurricane, formed

December 1940 - May 1941. 1 Sdn, RCAF, Hurricane, February 1941 - March 1941, renamed 401 Sdn, March 1941 - October 1941. 409 Sdn, Defiant, June 1941 - July 1941. 411 Sdn, Spitfire, June 1941 - November 1941. 412 Sdn, Spitfire, June 1941 - October 1941. 92 Sdn, Spitfire, October 1941 - February 1942. 609 Sdn, Spitfire, November 1941 - March 1942. 12 Gp Army Co-operation Flight, August 1941 - November 1941 renamed 288 Sdn, Hurricane and Oxford, November 1941 - December 1942. 411 Sdn, Spitfire, March 1942 - June 1942. 601 Sdn, Spitfire, March 1942 - April 1942. 421 Sdn, Spitfire, April 1942 - May 1942. 54 Sdn, Spitfire, June 1942. 411 Sdn, Spitfire, June 1942 - August 1942, August 1942 - March 1943. 242 Sdn, Spitfire, September 1942 - October 1942. 198 Sdn, Typhoon, December 1942 - January 1943. 288 Sdn, various types, January 1943 - November 1943, November 1943 - January 1944. 402 Sdn, Spitfire, March 1943 - August 1943. 411 Sdn, Spitfire, March 1943. 19 Sdn, Spitfire, May 1943 - June 1943. 167 Sdn, Spitfire, May 1943. 416 Sdn, Spitfire, June 1943 - August 1943. 349 Sdn, Spitfire, August 1943. 350 Sdn, Spitfire, August 1943 - October 1943. 402 Sdn, Spitfire, September 1943 - February 1944. 416 Sdn, Spitfire, October 1943 - February 1944. 438 Sdn, Hurricane, formed November 1943 - December 1943. 441 Sdn, Spitfire, formed February 1944 - March 1944. 442 Sdn, Spitfire, formed February 1944 - March 1944. 443 Sdn, Spitfire, formed February 1944 - March 1944. 402 Sdn, Spitfire, March 1944 - May 1944. 527 Sdn, various types for radar calibration, April 1944 - July 1945. 528 Sdn, various types for radar calibration, April 1944 - September 1944. 310 Sdn, Spitfire, July 1944 - August 1944. 116 Sdn, Oxford, 1944 - July 1945. 441 Sdn, Mustang, May 1945 - July 1945. 442 Sdn, Mustang, May 1945 - June 1945. 1 Officers Advanced Training School, July 1945 - 1947. RLG for Cranwell, 1946 - 1948. 1 Initial Training School, October 1948 - 1950. 2 Initial Training School, 1950 - September 1951. 2 Air Grading School, 1951 - February 1953. 399 SU January 1955 - present. 591 SU, July 1955 - present. 54 SU, February 1969 - present. Aerial Erectors School, September 1959 - present. Still open.

DONNA NOOK. Sheet 113 NGR 425979. Opened 1940? RLG for North Coates to 1945. Closed 1945

DONNA NOOK RANGE. Sheet 113 NGR 430996. Opened 1926. Gunnery and bombing range, 1926 - 1946? Closed 1946? Reopened August 1976. Still in use.

DUNHOLME LODGE. Sheet 121 NGR 993776. Opened May 1943. 44 Sdn, Lancaster, May 1943 - September 1944. 619 Sdn, Lancaster, April 1944 - September 1944. 170 Sdn, Lancaster, October 1944 - November 1944. Hamilcar glider modifications November 1944 - 1945. Closed 1945. Reopened 1959? 141 Sdn, Bloodhound SAM 1, 1959 - 1964. Closed 1964?

EAST KIRKBY. Sheet 122 NGR 341607. Opened August 1943. 57 Sdn, Lancaster, August 1943 - disb November 1945. 630 Sdn, Lancaster, formed November 1943 - disb July 1945. 460 Sdn, Lancaster, July 1945 - disb October 1945. Closed 1945. USAF 1954 - 1958. Closed 1958.

ELSHAM. Sheet 112 NGR 035135. Opened December 1916. 33 Sdn, C Flight, FE2, Avro 504, F2b. December 1916 - June 1919. Closed 1919.

ELSHAM WOLDS. Sheet 112 NGR 035135. Opened July 1941. 103 Sdn, Wellington, Halifax/Lancaster (1942), July 1941 - disb November 1945. 576 Sdn, Lancaster, formed November 1943 - October 1944. 21 Heavy Glider Conversion Unit, Albemarle, Horsa, Dakota. December 1945 - December 1946. Closed 1947.

FALDINGWORTH. Sheet 121 NGR 030847. Opened October 1943. 1667 Heavy Conversion Unit, Halifax, October 1943 - February 1944. 300 Sdn, Lancaster, March 1944 - disb October 1946. 305 Sdn, Mosquito, October 1946 - disb January 1947. Closed October 1948. Reopened 1957. 92 MU, 1957 - November 1972. Closed November 1972.

FISKERTON. Sheet 121 NGR 039725. Opened January 1943. 49 Sdn, Lancaster, January 1943 - October 1944. 576 Sdn, Lancaster, October 1944 - disb September 1945. 150 Sdn, Lancaster, November 1944. FIDO equipped. Closed 1946. Reopened 1961. ROC 15 GP HQ.

FOLKINGHAM. Sheet 130 NGR 040290. Opened 1943. 313th TCG. USAAF, Dakota, February 1944 - February 1945. Closed 1945. Reopened April 1960. 223 Sdn, Thor ICBM, April 1960 - August 1963. Closed August 1963.

FREISTON. Sheet 131 NGR 385405. Opened September 1917. RNAS armament training for Cranwell. 1917 - 1918. 4 School of Aerial Fighting, DH5, SE5, formed April 1918 - July 1918 renamed 4 Fighting School July 1918 - disb March 1920. Closed 1920.

FULBECK. Sheet 121 NGR 890503. Opened 1940. RLG for Cranwell 1940 - 1942. 1485 Bomber Gunnery Flight, 1942 - 1943. Air Bomber Training Flight, Oxford, 1942 - 1943. 434th TCG USAAF, Dakota, October 1943 - December 1943. 442nd TCG, Dakota, March 1944 - June 1944. 49 Sdn, RAF, Lancaster, October 1944 - April 1945. Automatic Gun Laying Turret Flight, Lancaster, 1945. Closed. Reopened as RLG for Cranwell, 1954? - 1969? Closed 1970?

GAINSBOROUGH. Opened 1916. HQ 33 Sdn, December 1916 - June 1918. Closed 1918.

GOSBERTON. Sheet 131 NGR 240310. WWI emergency landing ground.

GOXHILL. Sheet 113 NGR 107210. Opened June 1942. USAAF 1st FG, Lightning P38, June 1942 - August 1942. 52nd FG, Spitfire, August 1942 - October 1942. 81st FG, Lightning P38, October 1942 - November 1942. 358th FG, Thunderbolt P47, October 1942 - November 1942. 78th FG, Lightning P38/Thunderbolt P47, December 1942 - April 1943. 353rd FG, Thunderbolt P47, June 1943 - August 1943. 356th FG, Thunderbolt P47, August 1943 - October 1943. 496th Fighter Training Group, Lightning P38 and Mustang P51, December 1943 - February 1945. Closed 1945.

45 *Aircraft of 3 FTS, Grantham, in 1934. Those nearest the camera are Armstrong-Whitworth Atlases, and behind them are early Avro Tutors.* (Flight International).

GRANTHAM. Sheet 130 NGR 935342. Originally called SPITALGATE. Opened 1916. 49 Reserve Sdn, Shorthorn, BE2, November 1916 - May 1917, renamed 49 Training Sdn, May 1917 - September 1917. 15 Training Sdn, Avro 504, RE8, BE2, Bristol Scout, September 1917 - August 1918. 11 Reserve Sdn, BE2, Avro 504, April 1917 - May 1917, renamed 11 Training Sdn, May 1917 - September 1917. 20 Training Sdn, DH6, RE8, September 1917 - 1918. 37 Training Sdn, Avro 504, FK3, RE8, September 1917 - August 1918. 15 TS and 37 TS disb to form 39 Training Depot Sdn, FK8, FE2, Avro 504K, July 1918 - 1919, renamed 39 Training Sdn, 1919 - 1920. 70 Sdn, Camel/Snipe, February 1919 - disb January 1920. 29 Sdn, SE5, August 1919 - disb December 1919. 43 Sdn, Snipe, September 1919 - disb December 1919. 6 FTS, no aircraft 1920 - May 1921. 39 Sdn, DH9A, February 1921 - January 1928. 100 Sdn, DH9A, Fawn (1924), February 1922 - August 1924. 3 FTS, April 1922 - August 1937. 113 Sdn, Hind, August 1937 - April 1938. 211 Sdn, Hind and Audax, formed August 1937 - August 1938. 106 Sdn, Battle, September 1938 - October 1938. 185 Sdn, Battle, September 1938 - October 1938. 12 SFTS, October 1938 - 1942, renamed 12(P)AFU, 1942 - February 1945. 5 Group Communications Flight 1938 - November 1943, 17 SFTS, Oxford, 1945 - 1947 renamed 1 FTS, Harvard, 1947 - disb February 1948. RAF Officer Cadet Training Unit, March 1948 - March 1954. RAF Mess Staff School, September 1949 - August 1957.

HQ 24 Group, Tech Training Command, March 1954 - disb August 1957. RAF School of Education, August 1954 - November 1958. RAF Central Library, August 1955 to November 1958. Secretarial Officers School, 1959 - ? HQ 3 Police District, renamed HQ Provost and Security Services, 1959 - ? WRAF Depot 1960 - March 1974. Central Gliding School ? - 1975. Taken over by Royal Corps of Transport, as Prince William of Gloucester Barracks, 1975.

GRANTHAM 'ST VINCENTS'. Sheet 130 NGR 925351. Opened October 1937. HQ 5 Group, Bomber Command, October 1937 - November 1943. HQ, 9th Troop Carrier Command, USAAF, November 1943 - 1945. Care and Maintenance. Sold 1977.

GREENLAND TOP. Sheet 113 NGR 180115. Opened April 1918. 505 Flt, 251 Sdn, DH6, April 1918 - disb 1919. Closed 1919.

GRIMSBY. Sheet 113 NGR 273020. Civilian aerodrome. 25 ERFTS, Magister, Hind & Tiger Moth, formed June 1938 - disb September 1939. Closed for runway construction. Reopened November 1941. 142 Sdn, Wellington, November 1941 - December 1942. 100 Sdn, Lancaster, formed December 1942 - April 1945. 550 Sdn, Lancaster, formed November 1943 - January 1944. Used for storage. Closed after war. Sometimes known as WALTHAM.

GRIMSBY Tidal Basin. Sheet 113 NGR 275105. 22 MCU, formed 1940? - disb December 1945. Closed December 1945.

GRIMSTHORPE. Sheet 130 NGR 050230. WWI emergency landing ground. WWII bombing range.

HABROUGH. Sheet 113 NGR 148130. HQ 18 Group RAF, 1918.

HARLAXTON. Sheet 130 NGR 900320. Opened 1916. 44 Reserve Sdn, BE2, Avro 504, November 1916 - May 1917, renamed 44 Training Sdn, May 1917 - November 1917. 68 Sdn, DH5, formed January 1917 - September 1917. 98 Sdn, BE2, August 1917. 54 Reserve Sdn, DH6, Avro 504, March 1917 - May 1917, renamed 54 Training Sdn, May 1917 - 1918. 26 Training Sdn, RE8, DH4, FK3, BE2, DH6, September 1917 - 1918. 20 Training Sdn, DH6, RE8, 1918 - disb 1918. 53 Training Sdn, RE8, Avro 504, DH6, 1918 - disb 1918. 20 TS and 53 TS formed 40 Training Depot Station, DH6, RE8, Avro 504, 1918 - disb 1918. Closed 1919. Reopened June 1942, RLG for Grantham. Closed 1945.

HARPSWELL. See HEMSWELL.

HEMSWELL. Sheet 112 NGR 938903. Opened June 1918. Originally known, in World War I, as HARPSWELL. 199 (Night) Training Sdn, FE2, Sopwith 1½ Strutter, June 1918 - disb June 1919. Closed 1919. Reopened January 1937. 144 Sdn, Blenheim, Hampden (1939), February 1937 - July 1941. 61 Sdn, Anson Blenheim (1938), Hampden (1939), formed March 1937 - July 1941.

300 Sdn, Wellington, July 1941 - May 1942. 301 Sdn, Wellington, July 1941 - June 1943. 305 Sdn, Wellington, July 1942 - disb April 1943. Runways laid. 1 Lancaster Finishing School, January 1944 - disb November 1944. 150 Sdn, Lancaster, November 1944 - disb November 1945. 170 Sdn, Lancaster, November 1944 - disb November 1945. 1687 Bomber Defence Flight, Spitfire and Hurricane, April 1945 - disb October 1946. 109 Sdn, Mosquito, November 1945 - November 1946. 139 Sdn, Mosquito, February - November 1946. 83 Sdn, Lincoln, October 1946 - December 1955. 97 Sdn, Lincoln, November 1946 - April 1948, June 1948 - disb December 1955. 231 OCU, Mosquito, 1947 - October 1951. 109 Sdn, Mosquito, Canberra (1953), March 1950 - January 1956. 139 Sdn, Mosquito, Canberra (1953), April 1950 - January 1956. 199 Sdn, Mosquito, April 1952 - October 1952. 542 Sdn, Canberra PR7, April 1957 - July 1958. Thor ICBM Complex HQ 1958 - 1963. 97 Sdn, Thor ICBM, 1959 - disb May 1963, 2 Wing of 7 S of RT, Swinderby, 1964 - 1967. Closed 1967.

HIBALDSTOW. Sheet 112 NGR 976004. Opened May 1941. 255 Sdn, Defiant, May 1941 - September 1941. 253 Sdn, Hurricane, September 1941 - May 1942. 538 Sdn, Havoc, September 1941 - disb January 1943. 253 Sdn, Hurricane, May 1942 - June 1942, July 1942 - August 1942, August 1942 - November 1942. 532 Sdn, Havoc, September 1942 - disb February 1943. RLG for Kirton-in-Lindsey, May 1943 - 1945. Closed 1945.

HOLBEACH RANGE. Sheet 131 NGR 450310. Bombing and gunnery range, opened 1928, still in use. A small landing ground also existed.

HUMBERSTON. Sheet 113 NGR 290053. WWII WT station.

IMMINGHAM. Sheet 113 NGR 183140. Opened ? RNAS 8 KBS ? - April 1918, RAF 8 Balloon Station, April 1918 - disb 1919. Closed 1919.

INGHAM. Sheet 121 NGR 958830. Opened May 1942. 300 Sdn, Wellington, May 1942 - January 1943. 199 Sdn, Wellington, February 1943 - June 1943. 305 Sdn, Wellington, June 1943 - September 1943. 300 Sdn, Wellington, June 1943 - March 1944. 1687 Bomber Defence Training Flight, Spitfire and Hurricane, formed December 1944 - December 1944. Closed 1945? Sometimes called CAMMERINGHAM.

INGOLDMELLS. Sheet 122 NGR 560690. Opened 1940. Chain Home Low radar station. Closed 194?

KELSTERN. Sheet 113 NGR 255917. WWI emergency landing ground. Opened October 1943. 625 Sdn, Lancaster, formed October 1943 - April 1945. 170 Sdn, Lancaster, formed October 1944 - October 1944. Closed 1945.

KILLINGHOLME. Sheet 113 NGR 166203. Opened August 1914. RNAS seaplane station August 1914 - July 1918. USN flying boat base July 1918 - January 1919. 228 Sdn, Curtis H12, January - disb June 1919. 249 Sdn, Short 184, 1919 - disb October 1919. Closed 1919.

KIRMINGTON. Sheet 112 NGR 092095. Opened 1942. 15(P)AFU, Oxford 1942. 150 Sdn, Wellington, October 1942 - January 1943. 142 Sdn, Wellington, November 1942 - January 1943. 166 Sdn, Wellington/Lancaster, formed January 1943 - disb November 1945. 153 Sdn, Lancaster, formed October - October 1944. Closed 1945.

KIRTON-IN-LINDSEY. Sheet 112 NGR 943965. Opened December 1916. 33 Sdn, B Flt, FE2, December 1916 - June 1918. 33 Sdn, HQ and B Flt, Avro 504 and F2b, June 1918 - disb June 1919. Closed 1919. Reopened May 1940. 222 Sdn, Hurricane, May 1940. 65 Sdn, Spitfire, May 1940 - June 1940. 253 Sdn, Hurricane, May 1940 - July 1940. 264 Sdn, Defiant, July 1940 - August 1940, August 1940 - October 1940. 74 Sdn, Spitfire, August 1940 - September 1940. 307 Sdn, Defiant, September 1940 - November 1940. 616 Sdn, Spitfire, September 1940 - February 1941. 71 Sdn, Hurricane, November 1940 - April 1941. 255 Sdn, Defiant NF, formed November 1940 - May 1941. 85 Sdn, Hurricane, October 1940 - November 1940. 65 Sdn, Spitfire, February 1941 - October 1941. 452 Sdn, Spitfire, formed April 1941 - July 1941. 121 Sdn, Hurricane/Spitfire, formed May 1941 - December 1941. 136 Sdn, Hurricane, formed August 1941 - November 1941. 616 Sdn, Spitfire, September 1941 - January 1942. 611 Sdn, Spitfire, October 1941 - 1942. 133 Sdn, Spitfire, December 1941 - March 1942. 486 Sdn, Hurricane, March 1942 - April 1942. 306 Sdn, Spitfire, May 1942 - June 1942. 457 Sdn, Spitfire, May 1942 - June 1942. 303 Sdn, Spitfire, June 1942 - February 1943. 1st FG, USAAF, Lightning P38, June 1942 - August 1942. 43 Sdn, Hurricane, September 1942 - October 1942. 302 Sdn, Spitfire, February 1943 - April 1943. 317 Sdn, Spitfire, February 1943 - April 1943. 53 OTU, Spitfire, May 1943 - May 1945. 7 SFTS, Oxford, April 1946 - 1948. Central Synthetic Training Est and Aircrew Transit Unit, 1948 - 1949. Aircrew Educational School 1949 - 1950. Link Trainer School, 1950 - 1952. 2 Initial Training School, Tiger Moth, 1952, renamed 1 ITS 1954 - 1957. Care and Maintenance 1957 - 1960. 2 Gliding Centre 1960 - 1965. 7 School of Technical Training, 1960 - December 1965. Transferred to Royal Artillery, December 1965.

LANGTOFT. Sheet 130 NGR 138109. GCI radar station, opened 194? Closed 1950s.

LEADENHAM. Sheet 121 NGR 960520. Opened September 1916. One Flight 38 Sdn, FE2, September 1916 - May 1918. A Flight, 90 Sdn, Avro 504/Dolphin, May 1918 - disb June 1919. Closed 1919.

LINCOLN WEST COMMON. Sheet 121 NGR 960720. Opened 1917? 4 AAP 1917 - 1918. Closed 1919.

LUDFORD MAGNA. Sheet 113 NGR 202871. Opened June 1943. 101 Sdn, Lancaster, June 1943 - October 1945. FIDO equipped. Closed 1945. Reopened July 1959. 104 Sdn, Thor ICBM, formed July 1959 - disb May 1963. Closed May 1963.

46 *'Mudford-Magna' living up to its reputation; an evocative photo of G-George, 101 Sdn, on a winters day during WWII — note the FIDO pipes running alongside the runway. (101 Sdn).*

47 *The 'Macaws' aerobatic team on approach to Manby. These Hunting Jet Provost T4s were from the College of Air Warfare (CAW), hence the team's title. (P H T Green).*

MANBY. Sheet 122 NGR 383862. Opened August 1938. 1 Air Armament School, August 1938 - July 1944, renamed Empire Central Armament School, July 1944 - November 1944, renamed Empire Air Armament School, November 1944 - July 1949. RAF Flying College, formed July 1949 - July 1962, renamed College of Air Warfare, July 1962 - December 1973. School of Refresher Flying, 196? - December 1973. Closed March 1974.

MARKET DEEPING. Sheet 142 NGR 130100. WWI emergency landing ground.

MARKET STAINTON. Sheet 122 NGR 230802. Opened January 1943. 233 MU, January 1943 - 1948? Closed 1948?

METHERINGHAM. Sheet 121 NGR 100600. Opened October 1943. 106 Sdn, Lancaster, November 1943 - disb February 1946. 467 Sdn, Lancaster, June 1945 - disb September 1945. 189 Sdn, Lancaster, October 1945 - disb November 1945. FIDO equipped. Closed 1946.

MOORBY. Sheet 122 NGR 290644. WWI emergency landing ground.

MORTON HALL. Sheet 121 NGR 879642. Opened 194? Aircrew Commando School 1940? - November 1943. 5 Group HQ, November 1943 - disb December 1945. 21 Group HQ, 1947? - 1955. Closed 1955?

NEW HOLLAND. Sheet 112 NGR 080230. WWI emergency landing ground.

NOCTON HALL. Sheet 121 NGR 065640. RAF Hospital, opened 1947. Still in use.

NORTH COATES. Sheet 113 NGR 366018. Opened 1918. 404 Flight 248 Sdn, Short 225/Baby, 1918 - disb March 1919. Closed 1919. Reopened summers only for Armament Practice Camp, 1927 - 1935. 2 Armament Training Camp, formed 1935 - 1937. Air Observers School, formed January 1936 - 1937. 2 ATC plus AOS formed 2 Air Armament School, 1937 - March 1938, renamed 1 Air Observers School, March 1938 - September 1939. 1 Ground Defence School, 1939 - 1941. 236 Sdn, Blenheim IVF, February 1940 - May 1940. 235 Sdn, Blenheim IVF, February 1940 - May 1940. 248 Sdn, Blenheim IVF, March 1940 - April 1940. 812 Sdn, FAA, Swordfish, May 1940 - May 1941. 22 Sdn, Beaufort, April 1940 - April 1941. 42 Sdn, Beaufort, April 1941 - June 1941. 816 Sdn, FAA, Swordfish, May 1941 - June 1941. 86 Sdn, Beaufort, June 1941 - February 1942. 407 Sdn, Hudson, July 1941 - February 1942. 6 AACU, Lysander, October 1941 - 1942. 59 Sdn, Hudson, February 1942 - October 1942. 278 Sdn, Lysander, 1942. 53 Sdn, Hudson, February 1942 - May 1942. 415 Sdn, Hampden TB, June 1942 - August 1942, September 1942 - October 1942. 236 Sdn, Beaufighter, October 1942 - May 1945. 143 Sdn, Beaufighter, August 1942 - August 1943. 254 Sdn, Beaufighter, Mosquito (1945), October 1942 - June 1945. 143 Sdn, Beaufighter, February 1944 - May 1944, September 1944 - October 1944. 15 School of Technical Training, 1945 - ? 54 MU 194? - 1956?. 1 Initial Training School, 1952. Rebuilt as first

Bloodhound SAM base. Reopened 1958. 264 Sdn, Bloodhound SAM, April 1958 - 1962. 25 Sdn, Bloodhound SAM 2, October 1963 - 1971. Closed February 1971. Reopened 1976. B Flight of 85 Sdn, Bloodhound SAM 2, 1976 - present. Still open.

48 *North Coates airfield in 1937. The large aircraft in the left hand row is an Avro Anson and in the third row from the left a Boulton Paul Overstrand. On the right are three Saro Cloud amphibians. The smaller aircraft are assorted Westland Wallaces and Hawker Harts or Hinds.* (W/Cdr S Threapleton via P H T Green).

NORTH KILLINGHOLME. Sheet 113 NGR 124167. Opened November 1943. 550 Sdn, Lancaster, November 1943 - disb October 1945. Closed 1945.

NORTH WITHAM. Sheet 130 NGR 940220. Opened 1943. 1st Tactical Air Depot, USAAF, September 1943 - 1945. 9th Troop Carrier Pathfinder Group, Dakota, 1944. RAF storage. Closed 194?

NORTON DISNEY. Sheet 121 NGR 868643. Originally called SWINDERBY. Opened August 1939, 93 MU, August 1939 - 1950s. Closed 1950s.

ORBY. Sheet 122 NGR 498675. GCI radar station, opened 1941? Closed August 1945.

RAUCEBY. Sheet 130 NGR 040440. RAF Hospital. Opened 1940. Closed 1947.

SANDTOFT. Sheet 112. NGR 750075. Opened February 1943. 1667 HCU, Halifax, Lancaster (1945), February 1943 - disb November 1945. Closed 1945.

SCAMPTON. Sheet 121. NGR 957789. Opened December 1916. Originally called BRATTLEBY. 37 Reserve Sdn, November 1916 - April 1917, A Flight 33 Sdn, FE2, Bristol F2b (1918), Avro 504 (1918), December 1916 - June 1919. 60 Reserve Sdn, Avro 504, Pup, RE8, April 1917 - May 1917. Renamed 60 Training Sdn, May 1917 - July 1918. 81 Sdn, July 1917 - July 1918. 11 Training Sdn, BE2, Avro 504, Pup, Elephant, September 1917 - July 1918. 60 TS, 81 Sdn, and 11 TS merged to form 34 Training Depot Station, Pup, Dolphin, Avro 504, Camel, Scout, July 1918 - April 1919. Closed 1920. Reopened August 1936. 9 Sdn, Heyford, October 1936 - March 1938. 214 Sdn, Heyford, October 1936 - April 1937. 148 Sdn, Audax, Wellesley (1938), formed June 1937 - March 1938. 49 Sdn, Hampden, Manchester (1942), Lancaster (1943), March 1938 - January 1943. 83 Sdn, Hampden, Manchester (1941), Lancaster (1942), March 1938 - January 1940, March 1940 - August 1942. 98 Sdn, Battle, March 1940. 1518 BAT Flt, Oxford, formed November 1941 - 1943? 57 Sdn, Manchester/Lancaster, September 1942 - August 1943. 467 Sdn, Lancaster, formed November 1942 - November 1942. 617 Sdn, Lancaster, formed March 1943 - August 1943. Closed August 1943, runways laid. Reopened October 1944. 153 Sdn, Lancaster, formed October 1944 - disb September 1945. 1687 Bomber Defence Training Flight, Spitfire and Hurricane, December 1944 - April 1945. 625 Sdn, Lancaster, April 1945 - disb October 1945. 57 Sdn, Lancaster/Lincoln, December 1945 - May 1946. 100 Sdn, Lancaster, December 1945 - May 1946. 1 Group Major Servicing Unit, May 1946 - disb June 1948. Bomber Command Instructors School, January 1947 - July 1948 renamed Bomber Command Instrument Rating and Examing Flight, July 1948 - May 1953. 28 BW, USAF, B29, July - October 1948. 301 BW, USAF, B29, October 1948 - February 1949. 230 OCU, Lincoln, February 1949 - disb May 1953. 10 Sdn, Canberra, formed January 1953 - May 1955. 27 Sdn, Canberra, formed June 1953 - May 1955. 18 Sdn, Canberra, formed August 1953 - May 1955. 21 Sdn, Canberra, formed September 1953 - June 1955. Closed for reconstruction. RLG for Swinderby. 617 Sdn, Vulcan, formed May 1958 - present. 83 Sdn, Vulcan, formed October 1960 - disb July 1969. 27 Sdn, Vulcan, formed April 1961 - disb March 1972. 230 OCU, Vulcan and Hastings (1972-1977), December 1969 - present. 27 Sdn, Vulcan SR, formed November 1973 - present. 35 Sdn, Vulcan, January 1975 - present. Still open.

SCOPWICK. See DIGBY.

SKEGNESS. Opened August 1914. RNAS. Closed August 1914.

SKEGNESS. Opened February 1941. 11 Recruit Centre, February 1941 - disb October 1944. Closed October 1944.

49 *The 'Flying Elephant' badge of 27 Sdn is displayed on Vulcan SR2, XJ 782, as it climbs away from Scampton. The SR2 is outwardly identical to the B2.* (P H T Green).

SKELLINGTHORPE. Sheet 121 NGR 925688. Opened November 1941. 50 Sdn, Hampden, Manchester (1942), November 1941 - June 1942. RLG for Swinderby. 50 Sdn, Lancaster, October 1942 - June 1945. 61 Sdn, Lancaster, April 1944 - June 1945. 619 Sdn, Lancaster, June 1945 - disb July 1945. 463 Sdn, Lancaster, July 1945 - disb September 1945. RLG for Swinderby. 58 MU, 1946? - 1952? Closed 1952?

SKENDLEBY. Sheet 122. NGR 438708. Chain Home Low radar station. Opened 194? - Closed ?

SOUTH CARLTON. Sheet 121. NGR 965762. Opened November 1916. 45 Reserve Sdn, Farman, FB5, November 1916 - May 1917, renamed 45 Training Sdn, DH5, May 1917 - July 1918. 61 Training Sdn, DH6, FK8, May 1917 - July 1918. 39 Training Sdn, RE8, DH6, Avro 504, September 1917 - July 1918. 39 TS and 46 TS merged to form 46 Training Depot Station, Camel, Dolphin, 504, July 1918 - 1919, renamed 46 Training Sdn, Camel, Dolphin, 1919 - disb April 1920. 25 Sdn, DH4, September 1919 - December 1919. 57 Sdn, DH4, September 1919 - disb December 1919. Closed 1920.

SOUTH ELKINGTON. Sheet 113 NGR 300880. WWII WT Station.

SOUTH WITHAM. Sheet 130 NGR 915195. Opened March 1942. 100 MU, March 1942 - 195? Closed 195?

SPILSBY. Sheet 122 NGR 450645. Opened September 1943. 207 Sdn, Lancaster, October 1943 - October 1945. 44 Sdn, Lancaster, September 1944 - July 1945. 75 Sdn, Lancaster, July 1945 - disb October 1945. 2 Armament Practice School, 1945 - November 1946. Closed 1946. Reopened June 1955, USAF non-flying units, June 1955 - March 1958. Closed 1958.

SPITALGATE. See GRANTHAM.

STENIGOT. Sheet 122 NGR 257825. Chain Home radar station, opened 1939. Now Royal Corps of Signals.

STRUBBY. Sheet 122 NGR 440810. Opened April 1944. 280 Sdn, Warwick, April 1944 - September 1944. 144 Sdn, Beaufighter, July 1944 - September 1944. 404 Sdn, Beaufighter, July 1944 - September 1944. 619 Sdn, Lancaster, September 1944 - June 1945. 227 Sdn, Lancaster, April 1945 - June 1945. Closed September 1945. Reopened July 1949. RLG for Manby, July 1949 - September 1972. Closed September 1972.

STURGATE. Sheet 121 NGR 873873. Opened 1944. RLG for Blyton, 1944 - June 1945. 50 Sdn, Lancaster, June 1945 - January 1946. 61 Sdn, Lancaster, June 1945 - January 1946. Closed 1946. Reopened July 1952. USAF, July 1952 - 1964. 508 SFW, F84F, 1954. Closed 1964.

SUTTON BRIDGE. Sheet 131 NGR 476194. Opened 1926. Summer Armament Practice Camp, 1926 - 1936. 3 Armament Training Station, 1936 - September 1939. 64 Sdn, Blenheim 1F, August 1939. 266 Sdn, Battle, Spitfire (1940), formed October 1939 - March 1940. 264 Sdn, formed November - November 1939. 6 OTU, Hurricane, formed March 1940 - November 1940, renamed 56 OTU, November 1940 - March 1942. Central Gunnery School, March 1942 - February 1944. 7(P)AFU, Oxford, August 1944 - May 1945, renamed 7 FTS, May 1945 - April 1946. Closed 1946.

SWINDERBY. (Bomb Dump). See NORTON DISNEY.

SWINDERBY. Sheet 121 NGR 873615. Opened July 1940. 300 Sdn, Battle, Wellington (1940), August 1940 - July 1941. 301 Sdn, Battle, Wellington (1940), August 1940 - July 1941. 455 Sdn, Hampden, formed June 1941 - February 1942. 50 Sdn, Hampden, July 1941 - November 1941. 50 Sdn, Manchester/Lancaster, June 1942 - October 1942. 1654 HCU, Lancaster/Manchester, formed May 1942 - June 1942. 1660 HCU, Manchester/Halifax, Stirling (1943), Lancaster (1944), formed October 1942 - November 1946. 17 OTU, Wellington, November 1946 - May 1947, renamed 201 AFS, Wellington, Varsity (1951), May 1947 - June 1954, renamed 11 FTS Varsity, June 1954 - disb June 1955. 204 AFS, Mosquito, June 1950 - February 1953. 21 Group Comm Flight, May 1947 - November 1954. 8 FTS, Vampire, July 1955 - June 1964. Closed for flying. 7 School of Recruit Training, January 1964 - July 1970, renamed School of Recruit Training, July 1970 - present. Still open.

SWINSTEAD. Sheet 130 NGR 015230. WWI emergency landing ground.

THEDDLETHORPE. Sheet 113 NGR 469905. Opened 1935. Bombing and gunnery range. 1935 - December 1973. Closed December 1973. A small landing ground also existed.

TYDD ST MARY. Sheet 131 NGR 455185. Opened August 1917. B Flt. 51 Sdn, Avro 504, Camel, August 1917 - May 1919. Closed May 1919.

WADDINGTON. Sheet 121 NGR 982630. Opened November 1916. 47 Reserve Sdn, Shorthorn, November 1916 - May 1917, renamed 47 Training Sdn, Shorthorn, May 1917 - disb 1918. 48 Reserve Sdn, Shorthorn, November 1916 - May 1917, renamed 48 Training Sdn, Shorthorn, DH6, RE8, May 1917 - disb 1918. 51 Training Sdn, BE2, RE8, FE2, May 1917 - October 1918. 75 Training Sdn, DH4, formed November 1917 - December 1917. 47 TS and 48 TS merged to form 48 Training Depot Station, DH6, DH9, 1918 - 1919, renamed 48 Training Sdn, DH9A, 1919 - disb 1920. 23 Sdn, Dolphin, March 1919 - disb December 1919. 203 Sdn, Camel, March 1919 - December 1919. 204 Sdn, Camel, February 1919 - disb December 1919. Closed. Reopened 1926. 503 Sdn, Fawn, Hyderabad (1929), Hinaidi (1930), Wallace (1935), Hart (1936), Hind (1938), formed October 1926 - disb November 1938. 50 Sdn, Hind, Hampden (1939), formed May 1937 - July 1940. 110 Sdn, Hind, formed May

50 *A further example of 503 Sdn equipment is this Westland Wallace, over its home territory in 1936.* (P H T Green).

1937 - May 1939. 44 Sdn, Hind/ Blenheim, Hampden (1939), Lancaster (1941), June 1937 - May 1943. 88 Sdn, Hind, formed June 1937 - July 1937. 142 Sdn, Battle, June 1940 - July 1940. 207 Sdn, Manchester, formed November 1940 - November 1941. 97 Sdn, Manchester, February 1941 - March 1941. 420 Sdn, Hampden, formed December 1941 - August 1942. 6 Beam Approach Training Flight, Hampden, 1940 - November 1941, renamed 1506 BATF, November 1941 - 1943. 9 Sdn, Lancaster, August 1942 - April 1943. 1661 HCU, Lancaster, formed November 1942 - December 1942. Closed for runway construction. 1485 Bombing and Gunnery Flight, August 1943 - ? 463 Sdn, Lancaster, formed November 1943 - July 1945. 467 Sdn, Lancaster, formed November 1943 - June 1945. 617 Sdn, Lancaster, June 1945 - January 1946. 9 Sdn, Lancaster, July 1945 - January 1946. 50 Sdn, Lancaster, Lincoln (1947), January 1946 - August 1947, December 1947 - disb January 1951. 61 Sdn, Lancaster, Lincoln (1947), January 1946 - July 1947, December 1947 - December 1950. 12 Sdn, Lancaster, July 1946 - September 1946. 57 Sdn, Lincoln, October 1946 - October 1947, December 1947 - March 1950, July 1950 - March 1951, July 1951 - April 1953. 307 BW, USAF, B29, July 1948 - October 1948. 301 BW, USAF, B29, October 1948 - February 1949. 100 Sdn, Lincoln, March 1950 - June 1950, December 1950 - May 1952, August 1952 - August 1953. 49 Sdn, Lincoln, July 1952 - August 1953. Care and maintenance and reconstruction. Reopened May 1955. 27 Sdn, Canberra, May 1955 - October 1956, December 1956 - disb December 1957. 21 Sdn, Canberra, June 1955 - disb June 1957. 230 OCU, Vulcan, formed August 1956 - June 1961. 83 Sdn, Vulcan, formed July 1957 - October 1960. 44 Sdn, Vulcan, formed August 1960 - present. 101 Sdn, Vulcan, June 1961 - present. 50 Sdn, Vulcan, formed August 1961 - present. 9 Sdn, Vulcan, January 1975 - present. Still open.

WAINFLEET. Sheet 122 NGR 522570. Opened August 1938. Bombing and gunnery range. Still in use.

WALTHAM. See GRIMSBY.

WELLINGORE. Sheet 121 NGR 983540. Opened 193? RLG for Cranwell 193? - 1940. RLG for Digby 1940. 29 Sdn, Blenheim/Beaufighter, 1940 - April 1941. 402 Sdn, Hurricane, May 1941 - June 1941. 412 Sdn, Spitfire, October 1941 - May 1942. 154 Sdn, Spitfire, September 1942 - November 1942. 81 Sdn, Spitfire, October 1942. 288 Sdn, Blenheim, December 1942 - January 1943. 613 Sdn, Mustang, April 1943 - May 1943. 416 Sdn, Spitfire, May 1943 - June 1943. 349 Sdn, Spitfire, August 1943. 416 Sdn, Spitfire, September 1943 - October 1943. 439 Sdn, Hurricane, formed January 1944 - January 1944. 402 Sdn, Spitfire, February 1944 - March 1944. RLG for Cranwell. April 1944 - 1945. Closed 1945.

WICKENBY. Sheet 121 NGR 088803. Opened September 1942. 12 Sdn, Wellington/Lancaster, September 1942 - September 1945. 626 Sdn, Lancaster, formed November 1943 - disb October 1945. 109 Sdn, Mosquito, October 1945 - November 1945. Closed for flying. 92 MU, 1952 - June 1956. Closed June 1956.

WINTERTON. Sheet 112 NGR 920190. WWI emergency landing ground.

WOODHALL SPA. Sheet 122 NGR 204610. Opened February 1942. 97 Sdn, Lancaster, March 1942 - April 1943. 619 Sdn, Lancaster, formed April 1943 - January 1944. 617 Sdn, Lancaster, January 1944 - June 1945. 627 Sdn, Mosquito, April 1944 - renumbered 109 Sdn, Mosquito, October 1945 - October 1945. Closed. Reopened 1959? 112 Sdn, Bloodhound SAM, 1959? - 1965? Closed.

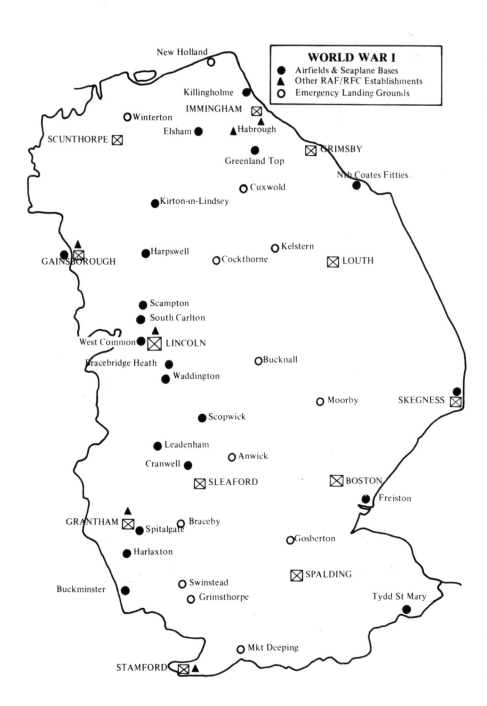

WORLD WAR I
● Airfields & Seaplane Bases
▲ Other RAF/RFC Establishments
○ Emergency Landing Grounds

New Holland

Killingholme

IMMINGHAM

Winterton

Elsham ●   ▲ Habrough

SCUNTHORPE

Greenland Top

GRIMSBY

Nth Coates Fitties

Cuxwold

Kirton-in-Lindsey

Kelstern

Harpswell   Cockthorne   LOUTH

GAINSBOROUGH

Scampton

South Carlton

West Common ● LINCOLN

Bracebridge Heath   Bucknall

Waddington

Moorby   SKEGNESS

Scopwick

Leadenham

Cranwell   Anwick

SLEAFORD   BOSTON

Freiston

GRANTHAM   Spitalgate   Braceby

Gosberton

Harlaxton

SPALDING

Buckminster   Swinstead

Grimsthorpe   Tydd St Mary

Mkt Deeping

STAMFORD

132

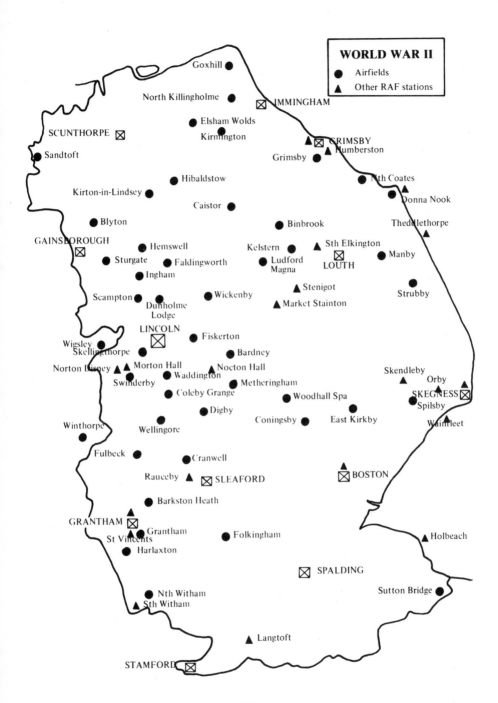

WORLD WAR II

● Airfields
▲ Other RAF stations

Goxhill ●

North Killingholme ●

⊠ IMMINGHAM

Elsham Wolds ●

SCUNTHORPE ⊠

Kirmington ●

▲ ⊠ GRIMSBY

Humberston

Sandtoft ●

Grimsby ●

Hibaldstow ●

Nth Coates ●

Kirton-in-Lindsey ●

Donna Nook ▲

Caistor ●

Blyton ●

Binbrook ●

Theddlethorpe ▲

GAINSBOROUGH ⊠

Hemswell ●

Kelstern ●

▲ Sth Elkington

Sturgate ●

Faldingworth ●

Ludford Magna ●

⊠ LOUTH

Manby ●

Ingham ●

Scampton ●

Wickenby ●

▲ Stenigot

Strubby ●

Dunholme Lodge ●

▲ Market Stainton

LINCOLN ⊠

Fiskerton ●

Wigsley ●

Skellingthorpe ●

Bardney ●

Norton Disney ▲▲

Morton Hall ●

▲ Nocton Hall

Skendleby ▲

Orby ●

Swinderby ●

Waddington ●

Metheringham ●

SKEGNESS ⊠ ▲

Coleby Grange ●

Woodhall Spa ●

Spilsby ●

Digby ●

Coningsby ●

East Kirkby ●

Wainfleet ▲

Winthorpe ●

Wellingore

Fulbeck ●

Cranwell ●

BOSTON ⊠ ▲

Rauceby ▲

⊠ SLEAFORD

Barkston Heath ●

GRANTHAM ⊠ ▲

Grantham ●

Folkingham ●

Holbeach ▲

St Vincents ▲

Harlaxton ●

SPALDING ⊠

Nth Witham ●

Sutton Bridge ●

▲ Sth Witham

▲ Langtoft

STAMFORD ⊠

133

Bibliography

The books listed fall into three categories — general histories of the RAF, those with special relevance to Lincolnshire, and those about aircraft types which have been based in the county in large numbers.

ALLWARD, M
Hurricane Special. Ian Allan 1975

BARKER, R
The Ship Busters. Chatto 1957

BARKER, R
The Thousand Plan. Chatto 1965

BEAUMAN, K B
Partners in Blue. The story of women's service with the Royal Air Force. Hutchinson 1971

BÈRE, R de la
A History of the Royal Air Force College Cranwell. Gale and Polden 1934

BOWYER, C
Airmen of World War I. Arms & Armour Press 1975

BOWYER, C
Beaufighter at War. Ian Allan 1976

BOWYER, C
The Flying Elephants. A history of 27 Sdn. MacDonald 1972

BOWYER, C
Hampden at War. Ian Allan 1976

BOWYER, C
History of the RAF. Hamlyn 1977

BOYLE, A
This Passing Glory. The full and authentic biography of Gp Capt Cheshire VC DSO DFC. Collins 1955

BOYLE, A
Trenchard. Collins 1962

BRAHAM, J R D
Scramble. Muller 1961

BRAMSON, A & BIRCH, N
The Tiger Moth Story (3rd ed). Air Review Ltd 1970

BRICKHILL, P
The Dam Busters (Rev ed). Evans Bros 1977

BRITISH air arms. A review of British Military Aviation. Merseyside Aviation Soc 1977

BUSHBY, J
Gunner's Moon. A memoir of the RAF night assault on Germany. Ian Allan 1972

CHARLWOOD, D E
No Moon Tonight. Angus & Robertson 1956

COOK, G F
The attacks on the Tirpitz. Ian Allan 1973

CROOKENDEN, N
Dropzone Normandy. Ian Allan 1976

CURRIE, J
Lancaster Target. New English Library 1977

DESTINY can wait. The Polish Air Force in the second world war. Heinemann 1949

E G
History of RAF Swinderby. RAF Swinderby (privately published) 1975

FIFTY years of Cranwell. A history of the Royal Air Force College 1920-1970. RAF College 1970

FINN, S
Lincolnshire Air War 1939-1945. Aero Litho Co 1973

FIRKINS, P C
Strike and Return. (460 Sdn) Paterson Brokensha Ltd, Perth, W A

GARBETT, M & GOULDING, B
The Lancaster at War. Ian Allan 1971

GENTIL, R
Trained to Intrude. Bachman & Turner 1974

GIBSON, G
Enemy Coast Ahead. Michael Joseph 1946

GOULDING, J. & MOYES, P J R
RAF Bomber Command and its Aircraft 1936-1940. Ian Allan 1975

GUNSTON, B
F-4 Phantom. Ian Allan 1977

HALL, R
Clouds of Fear. Bailey Bros & Swinen 1975

HALLEY, J J
Royal Air Force Unit Histories Vol 1 Nos 1 to 200 Squadrons. Air Britain 1969

HALLEY, J J
Royal Air Force Unit Histories Vol 2 Nos 201 to 1435 Squadrons. Air Britain 1973

HYDE, H M
British Air Policy Between the Wars 1918-1939. Heinemann 1976

JACKSON, R
Airships in Peace and War. Cassell 1971

JAMES, A G T
The Royal Air Force. The past 30 years. MacDonald & Janes 1976

JEFFORD, C G
A History of Basic Observer and Navigator Training since 1914. RAF Finningley 1972

JEFFORD, C G
A History of RAF Scampton 1917-1968. Delta Magazine 1968

LAWRENCE, T E
The Mint. Cape 1955

LAWRENCE, W J
No 5 Bomber Group RAF (1939-1945). Chivers 1970 (Faber 1951)

LONGMORE, A
From Sea to Sky 1910-1945. Bles 1946

LUMSDEN, A
Wellington Special. Ian Allen 1974

MASON, F K
Battle over Britain. MacWhirter 1969

MASON, T
The History of 9 Squadron, Royal Air Force. Beaumont 1965

MIDDLEBROOK, M
The Nuremberg Raid. Allen Lane 1973

MONTGOMERY, B G
A Short History of RAF Digby 1918 to 1973. RAF Digby 1973

MOYES, P J R
Bomber Squadrons of the RAF and their Aircraft (2nd ed.) MacDonald 1976

OFFENBERG, J H M
Lonely Warrior. Souvenir Press 1956

O, K M
Per Ardua. A short history of the Royal Air Force Regiment from 1942 to 1974. RAF Regiment 1974

POOLMAN, K
Zeppelins over England. Evans 1960

PRICE, A
Spitfire at War. Ian Allen 1974

RAWLINGS, J D R
Fighter Squadrons of the RAF and their Aircraft (2nd ed.) MacDonald 1976

REVIE, A
The Lost Command. Bruce & Watson 1971

RICHARDS, D & SAUNDERS, H St G
Royal Air Force 1939-1945 Vol I *The Fight at Odds.* HMSO 1953 Vol II *The Fight avails.* HMSO 1954 Vol III *The Fight is Won.* HMSO 1954

ROBERTSON, B
Beaufort Special. Ian Allan 1976

ROBERTSON, B
Lancaster - Story of a Famous Bomber. Harleyford 1964

ROBERTSON, B
The RAF. A pictorial history. Hale 1978

ROCHFORD, L H
I Chose the Sky. Kimber 1977

SHARP, C & BOWYER, M J F
Mosquito. (2nd ed) Faber 1971

SHORES, C & WILLIAMS, C
Aces High. The fighter aces of the British and Commonwealth Air Forces in World War II. Spearman 1966

STORY of 11 Group Royal Observer Corps. John Newton 1946

STRANGE, L A
Recollections of an Airman. Hamilton 1933

TAYLOR, J W R & MOYES, P J R
Pictorial History of the RAF Vol I 1918-1939. Ian Allan 1968
Vol II 1939-1945 Ian Allan 1969
Vol III 1945-1969 Ian Allan 1970

TEDDER, Lord
With Prejudice. Cassell 1966

THETFORD, O
Aircraft of the Royal Air Force since 1918 (6th ed). Putnam 1976

THETFORD, O
British Naval Aircraft since 1912. Putnam 1971

TREDREY, F D
Pioneer Pilot. The great Smith-Barry who taught the world how to fly. Peter Davies 1976

VERRIER, A
The Bombing Offensive. Batsford 1968

WAINWRIGHT, J
Tail-end Charlie. MacMillan 1978

WALLS, J
Clayton and Shuttleworth and Marshall aircraft production. Control Column 1977
Robey Aircraft Production. Aero Litho 1975
Ruston Aircraft Production. Aero Litho 1974

WEBSTER, C & FRANKLAND, N
The Strategic Air Offensive against Germany 1939-1945. Vols I-IV. HMSO 1961

WHEELER, A
Flying between the Wars. Foulis 1972

WHITE, A N
44 (Rhodesia) Squadron on Operations. A N White 1977

WHITTLE, F
Jet. The story of a pioneer. Muller 1953

WOOD, D
Attack Warning Red. The Royal Observer Corps and the defence of Britain 1925-1975. MacDonald & Janes 1976

Index

This index covers all British and American Air Force Squadrons and other units mentioned in the text, together with place names and geographical areas in Lincolnshire. It does not include personal names or places and locations in other counties.

Part One - Locations

Alford 8
Anderby 8
Anderby Creek 83
Anwick 10, 112
Bardney 58, 65, 68, 70, 97, 112
Barkston Heath 53, 80, 85, 86, 104, 105, 108, 112
Belton Park 83, 112
Binbrook 45, 49, 60, 65, 68, 89, 90, 91, 92, 96 97, 100, 101, 102, 103, 104, 108, 112
Blankney Hall 37, 92, 113
Blyton 49, 76, 95, 113
Boston 4, 6, 62, 75, 82
Bourne 6
Bracebridge Heath 15, 113
Braceby 10, 113
Brattleby 9, 114
Brocklesby 74
Buckminster (airfield) 9, 114
Bucknall 10, 114
Caistor 56, 75, 80, 97, 114
Cammeringham 114
Cleethorpes 1, 2, 8, 62
Cockthorne 10, 114
Coleby Grange 37, 39, 77, 78, 97, 114
Coningsby 46, 58, 62, 65, 68, 89, 90, 91, 97 99, 102, 103, 104, 108, 109, 114
Cranwell 1, 5, 12, 15, 17, 23, 35, 52, 80, 93, 94 106, 107, 108, 110, 115
Cuxwold 10, 115
Denton 13
Digby 12, 19, 22, 23, 24, 32, 33, 35, 36, 76, 77 92, 93, 107, 108, 110, 115
Donington on Bain 75
Donna Nook 2, 26, 51, 95, 104, 108, 111, 116
Dunholme Lodge 58, 65, 66, 67, 72, 97, 116
East Halton 8
East Kirkby 58, 65, 68, 89, 95, 116
Elsham 9, 117
Elsham Wolds 49, 57, 65, 68, 73, 90, 117
Faldingworth 66, 68, 90, 95, 117
Firsby 87
Fiskerton 8, 57, 58, 65, 68, 70, 74, 84, 117
Folkingham 85, 86, 97, 117
Freiston 6, 7, 12, 117
Fulbeck 53, 68, 69, 71, 73, 80, 85, 86, 104, 105, 117
Gainsborough 4, 9, 117
Gonerby 75
Gosberton 10, 117
Goxhill 45, 75, 84, 117

Grantham 13, 24, 32, 35, 55, 58, 75, 80, 83, 85 94, 97, 107, 108, 118
Grantham 'St. Vincents' 32, 55, 58, 85, 119
Greenland Top 16, 119
Grimsby 3, 24, 49, 57, 65, 69, 74, 83, 119
Grimsthorpe 10, 119
Habrough 16, 119
Hackthorne 83
Hallington 75
Harlaxton 11, 12, 55, 80, 119
Harpswell 12, 119
Heminsby 74
Hemswell 31, 32, 33, 35, 45, 47, 48, 49, 57, 68, 73, 74, 89, 90, 91, 97, 98, 107, 119
Hibaldstow 44, 76, 77, 120
Holbeach 26, 32, 104, 108, 111, 120
Horncastle 6
Humberston 4, 8, 82, 120
Immingham 2, 4, 36, 120
Ingham 49, 57, 66, 67, 120
Ingoldmells 77, 82, 120
Keelby 16
Kelstern 10, 58, 65, 69, 120
Killingholme 1, 2, 8, 16, 120
Killingholme, North See North Killingholme
Kirkstead 61
Kirmington 49, 55, 57, 65, 66, 68, 121
Kirton-in-Lindsey 9, 33, 42, 56, 76, 82, 89, 94, 97, 108, 121
Langtoft 77, 82, 92, 121
Langworth 61
Leadenham 9, 121
Lincoln 15, 19, 43, 62, 69, 70, 83, 84, 121
Lissington 61
Louth 38, 56
Ludford Magna 58, 64, 65, 68, 72, 97, 121
Mablethorpe 2
Manby 28, 33, 35, 56, 82, 89, 92, 106, 123
Market Deeping 10, 123
Market Stainton 74, 123
Metheringham 8, 60, 65, 68, 70, 87, 89, 90, 123
Moorby 10, 123
Morton Hall 58, 106, 123
Navenby 38
New Holland 10, 123
Nocton Hall 95, 108, 110, 123
North Coates 27, 35, 50, 78, 83, 89, 94, 97, 100, 104, 108, 110, 123
North Coates Fitties 16, 26
North Killingholme 60, 65, 68, 124
North Witham 85, 124

Norton Disney 74, 124
Orby 77, 78, 82, 124
Owmby 4
Quarrington 5
Rauceby 53, 95, 125
Sandtoft 76, 95, 125
Scampton 9, 11, 12, 13, 31, 32, 33, 35, 45, 48, 57, 58, 66, 67, 68, 70, 74, 89, 90, 91, 95, 97, 98, 99, 108, 110, 125
Scopwick 12, 17, 23, 39, 125
Skegness 2, 6, 38, 51, 61, 82, 87, 125
Skellingthorpe 8, 48, 57, 65, 68, 70, 89, 90, 126
Skendleby 77, 82, 126
Sleaford 5, 19
South Carlton 11, 12, 13, 15, 126
South Elkington 82, 126
South Witham 74, 126
Spilsby 60, 61, 65, 68, 87, 89, 90, 95, 127
Spitalgate 11, 12, 17, 23, 24, 127
Stamford 9
Stenigot 37, 72, 77, 82, 127
Strubby 68, 69, 79, 92, 106, 127
Sturgate 76, 89, 90, 95, 127
Sudbrooke 72
Sutton Bridge 6, 26, 28, 35, 54, 82, 89, 127
Swinderby 1, 46, 58, 69, 74, 75, 76, 89, 93, 95, 106, 107, 108, 111, 127
Swinstead 10, 128
Temple Bruer 21
Theddlethorpe 28, 73, 104, 128
Timberland 62
Tydd St Mary 10, 128
Uffington 8
Waddington 11, 12, 14, 29, 33, 35, 45, 50, 54, 57, 58, 61, 65, 66, 68, 70, 74, 84, 89, 90, 95, 96, 97, 98, 99, 107, 108, 111, 128
Wainfleet 32, 62, 104, 108, 111, 129
Waltham 129
Welbourn 8
Wellingore 21, 37, 77, 80, 129
Wickenby 49, 57, 65, 68, 95, 130
Winterton 10, 130
Withcall 75
Woodhall Spa 47, 48, 57, 61, 62, 68, 70, 97, 104, 130

Part Two - Units

Advanced Flying Schools 201 93, 127 202 93 204 93, 127
Aerial Erectors School 107, 108, 116
Air Armament Schools 1 28, 56, 82, 123 2 28
Air Bomber Training Flight 117
Aircraft Acceptance Park 4 15, 113, 121
Aircrew Commando School 58, 123
Aircrew Educational Unit 93, 121
Aircrew Transit Unit 93, 121
Air Experience Flight 7 107
Air Fighting Development Sdn 101, 113
Air Observers School 28, 123 1 28, 50, 123
Anti-Aircraft Co-operation Units 6 51, 123 7 51, 123

Armament Practice Camp 4 123
Armament Practice School 2 90, 127
Armament Training Schools 2 28, 123 3 28, 54, 127
Army Co-operation Flight 12 Group 116
Balloon Station 8 4, 120
Bases 51 75 52 58, 70 75 76, 93
Battle of Britain Memorial Flight 104, 108, 115
Beam Approach Training Flights 6 129 1506 129 1514 73, 114 1518 125 1536 80
Bomber Command Instructors School 125
Bomber Defence Training Flight 1687 67, 120, 125
Bomber Gunnery Flight 1485 117, 129
Central Fighter Establishment 100, 101, 113
Central Flying School 106, 109, 110, 115 2 53, 115
Central Gliding School 108, 119
Central Gunnery School 54, 82, 127
Central Link Trainer School 121
Central Synthetic Training Establishment 121
Electrical & Wireless School 1 19, 22, 53, 115
Elementary & Reserve Flying Training School 25 119
Elementary Flying Training Squadron 111
Empire Air Armament School 82, 123
Empire Central Armament School 82, 123
Equipment Officers School 93
Equipment Training School 21, 53, 115
Fighter Command Trials Unit 101, 113
Fighting School 4 12, 117
Fleet Air Arm Sdns 776 51, 123 812 50, 123 816 50, 123
Flying Instructors School 2 53, 115
Flying Selection Squadron 111
Flying Training Schools 1 23, 94, 107, 118 2 22, 24, 113 3 23, 32, 110, 115, 118 4 23 5 23 6 23, 118 7 94, 121, 127 8 106, 107, 127 11 94, 106, 127 19 93, 94, 115 Basic 110
Gliding Centre 2 108, 121
Grading School 2 93, 116
Ground Armament School 2 56
Ground Defence School 1 50, 83, 123
Groups 1 45, 48, 49, 57, 68, 69, 73, 76, 89, 91, 92, 95, 99 3 89, 90, 91, 95 4 60 5 32, 46, 47, 48, 49, 55, 57, 58, 62, 68, 69, 73, 74, 75, 76, 85, 89, 118, 119, 123 6 60 7 76 8 57 11 101, 103, 104 12 32, 41 18 16, 119 21 21, 53, 93, 106, 115, 123, 127 24 107, 119 25 106 38 102
Heavy Conversion Units 1654 75, 127 1660 75, 76, 93, 127 1661 75, 129 1662 76, 113 1667 76, 117, 125
Heavy Glider Conversion Unit 21 90, 117
HMS Daedalus 5, 115
HMS Killingholme 3
Initial Training Schools 1 93, 95, 116, 121, 123 2 93, 94, 116, 121
Initial Training Wings 1 94 3 115
Joint Services Trials Unit 17 100
Kite Balloon Section 8 4, 120

Lancaster Finishing Schools **1** 120 **5** 75
Lighting Training Flight 102, 108, 113
Maintenance Units **54** 95, 123 **58** 90, 126 **92** 95,
   99, 117, 130 **93** 74, 124 **100** 74, 126 **233** 74,
   123
Major Servicing Unit **1 Group** 125
Marine Craft Unit **22** 83, 119
Mess Staff School 107, 118
Motor Launch Unit **22** 51, 83
Officers Advanced Training School **1** 93, 116
Operational Conversion Units **228** 102, 103, 108,
   109, 114 **229** 109 **230** 91, 96, 99, 108, 110, 125,
   129 **231** 114, 120
Operational Training Units **3** 53, 80, 115 **6** 54,
   127 **17** 93, 127 **51** 55 **53** 76, 121 **56** 54, 127
(Pilots) Advanced Flying Units **7** 82, 127 **12** 80,
   81, 118 **15** 55, 121
Radio Schools **1** 53, 80, 94, 115 **6** 94 **8** 115
Recruit Centre **11** 82, 125
Recruit Training Pool **2** 50
Red Arrows 110
Reserve Sdns **11** 118 **37** 11, 125 **44** 11, 119 **45** 11,
   126 **47** 11, 128 **48** 128 **49** 11, 118 **54** 119 **60**
   125
Royal Air Force Aerobatic Team 110
Royal Air Force Apprentices School 115
Royal Air Force Cadet College 19, 115
Royal Air Force Central Library 71, 107, 119
Royal Air Force College 17, 94, 104, 108, 110, 115
Royal Air Force College of Air Warfare 106, 123
Royal Air Force Flying College 92, 106, 123
Royal Air Force Hospitals
   Cranwell 19, 53, 115
   Nocton Hall 95, 108, 110, 123
   Rauceby 53, 95, 125
Royal Air Force Officer Cadet Training Unit 107,
   118
Royal Air Force Police
   3 District HQ 108, 119
   Provost & Security Services HQ 108, 119
Royal Air Force Regiment Depot 83, 112
Royal Air Force School of Recruit Training 107,
   108, 111, 127
Royal Air Force Technical College 104
Royal Auxillary Air Force Regiment **2503 Sdn** 111
   2729 Sdn 111
Royal Observer Corps 83, 117
School of Clerks Accounting 22, 53, 115
School of Education 107, 119
School of Refresher Flying 106, 123
School of Stores Accountancy & Storekeeping 21,
   115
School of Aerial Fighting **4** 12, 117
School of Recruit Training **7** 107, 120, 127 **RAF**
   107, 108, 111, 127
Schools of Technical Training **5** 102 **7** 108, 121
   15 95, 123
Secretarial Branch Training Establishment 93
Secretarial Officers School 107, 119
Service Flying Training Schools **12** 25, 55, 80, 118
   17 80, 94, 115, 118 **19** 115 **RAF College**
   52, 80, 115
Signals School **1** 53, 115
Signals Units **54** 107, 108, 116 **399** 107, 108,
   116 **591** 107, 108, 116

Squadrons **5 Sdn** 100, 101, 108, 109, 113 **6 Sdn**
103, 115 **8 Sdn** 111 **9 Sdn** 31, 48, 57, 58, 63,
65, 68, 70, 90, 96, 97, 98, 99, 108, 111, 112,
114, 125, 129 **10 Sdn** 91, 125 **11 Sdn** 101, 102,
108, 109, 113, 115 **12 Sdn** 45, 46, 49, 57, 65,
68, 90, 92, 96, 97, 98, 112, 113, 114, 129, 130
15 Sdn 90, 114 **18 Sdn** 91, 125 **19 Sdn** 76, 116
21 Sdn 91, 96, 125, 129 **22 Sdn** 50, 123 **23 Sdn**
104, 115 **25 Sdn** 100, 108, 115, 124, 126 **27
Sdn** 91, 96, 98, 99, 108, 110, 125, 129 **29 Sdn**
37, 39, 103, 108, 109, 115, 118, 129 **33 Sdn**
9, 10, 117, 121, 125 **35 Sdn** 98, 108, 114, 125
38 Sdn 9, 114, 121 **39 Sdn** 23, 118 **40 Sdn** 114
41 Sdn 103, 115 **42 Sdn** 50, 123 **43 Sdn** 44,
118, 121 **44 Sdn** 30, 31, 35, 46, 47, 48, 57, 58,
65, 66, 68, 70, 90, 97, 98, 99, 111, 116, 127,
129 **45 Sdn** 97, 114 **46 Sdn** 32, 36, 37, 115
49 Sdn 31, 35, 46, 48, 57, 65, 68, 70, 117, 125,
129 **50 Sdn** 30, 31, 48, 57, 65, 68, 70, 90, 91,
98, 99, 108, 111, 112, 126, 127, 128, 129 **51
Sdn** 10, 128 **53 Sdn** 51, 123 **54 Sdn** 41, 103,
115, 116 **56 Sdn** 37, 104, 108, 114, 115 **57 Sdn**
48, 57, 58, 65, 68, 89, 90, 114, 116, 125, 126,
129 **59 Sdn** 51, 123 **61 Sdn** 31, 46, 48, 65, 68,
75, 90, 114, 119, 126, 127, 129 **64 Sdn** 54, 100,
113, 121 **65 Sdn** 42, 44, 121 **68 Sdn** 78, 114,
119 **70 Sdn** 118 **71 Sdn** 42, 44, 121 **73 Sdn**
33, 36, 115 **74 Sdn** 42, 121 **75 Sdn** 90, 127
79 Sdn 37, 115 **81 Sdn** 125, 129 **83 Sdn** 31,
35, 38, 46, 48, 54, 68, 70, 90, 91, 97, 98, 99,
114, 120, 125, 129 **85 Sdn** 42, 100, 101, 104,
108, 113, 121, 124 **86 Sdn** 50, 51, 123 **88 Sdn**
30, 31, 129 **90 Sdn** 9, 114, 121 **92 Sdn** 39, 116
97 Sdn 46, 47, 48, 57, 68, 75, 91, 114, 120, 129,
130 **98 Sdn** 119, 125 **100 Sdn** 23, 49, 57, 58,
65, 68, 72, 90, 91, 96, 98, 99, 108, 111, 112,
121, 129 **103 Sdn** 49, 57, 65, 68, 117 **104 Sdn**
121 **106 Sdn** 32, 46, 47, 60, 65, 68, 70, 75, 90,
112, 114, 118, 123 **109 Sdn** 90, 91, 96, 113,
114, 120, 130 **110 Sdn** 30, 31, 129 **111 Sdn**
37, 103, 104, 115 **112 Sdn** 97, 130 **113 Sdn**
32, 79, 118 **116 Sdn** 77, 116 **120 Sdn** 15, 113
121 Sdn 44, 121 **133 Sdn** 44, 121 **136 Sdn** 44,
121 **139 Sdn** 90, 91, 97, 112, 114, 120 **141 Sdn**
97, 116 **142 Sdn** 45, 46, 49, 112, 114, 119, 121,
129 **143 Sdn** 51, 78, 79, 123 **144 Sdn** 31, 35,
36, 46, 48, 119, 127 **145 Sdn** 40 **148 Sdn** 31,
125 **149 Sdn** 90, 114 **150 Sdn** 49, 68, 73, 117,
120, 121 **151 Sdn** 37, 115 **153 Sdn** 66, 68, 121,
125 **154 Sdn** 129 **166 Sdn** 57, 65, 68, 121 **167
Sdn** 76, 116 **170 Sdn** 68, 116, 120 **185 Sdn** 32,
118 **189 Sdn** 68, 112, 123 **198 Sdn** 42, 116
199 Sdn 12, 49, 57, 113, 119, 120 **203 Sdn** 115,
128 **204 Sdn** 128 **206 Sdn** 51 **207 Sdn** 46, 48,
60, 65, 68, 75, 127, 129 **209 Sdn** 115 **210 Sdn**
115 **211 Sdn** 32, 118 **213 Sdn** 115 **214 Sdn** 125
215 Sdn 37 **217 Sdn** 51 **222 Sdn** 3, 7, 42, 115,
121 **223 Sdn** 117 **224 Sdn** 51 **227 Sdn**
68, 127 **228 Sdn** 4, 120 **229 Sdn** 36, 115 **235
Sdn** 50, 123 **236 Sdn** 50, 51, 78, 83, 123 **242
Sdn** 41, 116 **248 Sdn** 16, 50, 123 **249 Sdn** 4,
97, 114, 120 **251 Sdn** 16, 119 **253 Sdn** 42, 44,
120, 121 **254 Sdn** 51, 78, 123 **255 Sdn** 42, 120,
121 **264 Sdn** 42, 54, 78, 97, 100, 114, 121,

124, 127 **266 Sdn** 54, 127 **269 Sdn** 114 **275 Sdn** 95 **278
Sdn** 51, 123 **280 Sdn** 79, 127 **288 Sdn** 42, 114, 116, 129
300 Sdn 46, 48, 49, 57, 66, 68, 90, 117, 120, 127 **301
Sdn** 46, 48, 49, 57, 120, 127 **302 Sdn** 76, 121 **303 Sdn**
44, 76, 121 **305 Sdn** 49, 57, 66, 90, 117, 120 **306 Sdn**
44, 121 **307 Sdn** 42, 78, 114, 121 **310 Sdn** 77, 116 **317
Sdn** 76, 121 **349 Sdn** 76, 77, 116, 129 **350 Sdn** 76, 116
401 Sdn 37, 116 **402 Sdn** 37, 76, 77, 115, 116 **404 Sdn**
79, 127 **407 Sdn** 50, 51, 123 **409 Sdn** 39, 42, 77, 114,
116 **410 Sdn** 77, 78, 114 **411 Sdn** 39, 76, 116 **412 Sdn**
39, 116, 129 **415 Sdn** 51, 123 **416 Sdn** 76, 116, 129 **420
Sdn** 48, 129 **421 Sdn** 41, 116 **438 Sdn** 76, 77, 116 **439
Sdn** 77, 129 **441 Sdn** 76, 77, 92, 116 **442 Sdn** 76, 77,
116 **443 Sdn** 76, 116 **452 Sdn** 44, 121 **455 Sdn** 48, 127
457 Sdn 44, 121 **460 Sdn** 60, 65, 68, 112, 116 **463 Sdn**
65, 66, 68, 126, 129 **467 Sdn** 48, 65, 66, 68, 123, 125,
129 **486 Sdn** 44, 121 **503 Sdn** 29, 36, 128 **504 Sdn** 36,
115 **527 Sdn** 77, 116 **528 Sdn** 77, 116 **532 Sdn** 45, 120
538 Sdn 44, 120 **542 Sdn** 120 **550 Sdn** 60, 65, 68, 119,
121 **576 Sdn** 65, 68, 73, 117 **601 Sdn** 41, 116 **602 Sdn**
36 **609 Sdn** 39, 40, 76, 116 **611 Sdn** 36, 44, 115, 121
613 Sdn 77, 129 **616 Sdn** 31, 42, 44, 121 **617 Sdn** 58,
62, 68, 70, 89, 90, 97, 98, 99, 108, 110, 112, 114, 125,
129, 130 **619 Sdn** 65, 66, 68, 114, 116, 126, 127, 130
625 Sdn 58, 65, 68, 120, 125 **626 Sdn** 65, 68, 130 **627
Sdn** 68, 130 **630 Sdn** 65, 68, 116 '**1066 Sdn**' 99
Stores Depot Part **6** 15
Supplies Depot **Cranwell** 21, 53, 115
Target Towing Flights **1 Group** 112 **5 Group** 114 **1481** 112
Training Depot Stations **34** 12, 13, 125 **39** 12, 118 **40** 12,
119 **46** 12, 13, 126 **48** 12, 128 **56** 12, 115 **57** 12, 115
58 12, 115 **59** 12, 115 **201** 12, 115 **202** 12, 115 **213** 12,
115
Training Sdns **11** 13, 118, 125 **15** 118 **20** 118, 119 **26** 119
37 118 **39** 118, 126 **44** 119 **45** 126 **46** 126 **47** 128 **48** 128
49 118 **51** 128 **53** 119 **54** 119 **59** 115 **60** 125 **61** 125 **75** 128
Training Wings **23** 13, 14 **24** 13 **59** 115
United States Air Force **28 BW** 90, 125 **301 BW** 90, 125,
129 **307 BW** 90, 129 **508 SFW** 95, 127
United States Army Air Force
  8th Air Force 45, 57, 84, 85 **1 FG** 44, 117, 121 **4 FG**
    42 **52 FG** 117 **78 FG** 84, 117 **81 FG** 117 **353 FG** 84,
    117 **356 FG** 84, 117 **358 FG** 117 **496 FTG** 84, 117
  9th Air Force 84, 112 **1 TAD** 85, 124 **9 TCC** 85, 86, 119
  9 TCC Pathfinder Group 85, 124 **61 TCG** 85, 86,
    112 **313 TCG** 85, 86, 117 **349 TCG** 86, 112 **434 TCG**
    85, 117 **442 TCG** 85, 86, 117 **52 TCW** 85
University Air Sdn **East Midlands** 107
Wireless Operators School 107, 115
Womens Royal Air Force Depot 108, 119

FISKERTON AIRFIELD

KEY TO MAP

Site 1   –   Airfield
,,   2   –   Bomb dump
,,   3   –   Officers Mess, Sgts Mess. C O's quarters
,,   4   –   Gymnasium, Chapel, NAAFI
,,   5   –   Living quarters, Airmens Mess
,,   6   –   Living quarters, Airmens Mess
,,   7   –   Living quarters, Sgts Mess, Airmens Mess
,,   8   –   Living quarters
,,   9   –   Sick quarters, mortuary, ambulance station
,,   10   –   Living quarters, Sgts Mess, Airmens Mess
,,   11   –   Living quarters, Sgts Mess, Airmens Mess
,,   12   –   Living quarters, Sgts Mess, Airmens Mess
,,   13   –   Sewage
,,   14   –   Living quarters, WAAF, WAAF Mess, WAAF NAAFI